CW00688176

DATE DUE

CINEMA BUILDERS

CINEMA BUILDERS

EDWIN HEATHCOTE

Ⓦ WILEY-ACADEMY

Acknowledgements

I would like to thank my wife Krisztina with whom I most enjoy going to the cinema and my mother and father who nurtured my love of films. I would also like to acknowledge the help of all the architects whose work appears in this book and those who photographed those buildings. Particular thanks go to Christian Richters, one of the world's finest architectural photographers, without whose images this book would have been virtually impossible.

Photographic credits

All photographs are courtesy of the architects or from the Architectural Press archive, unless stated otherwise; every effort has been made to locate sources and credit material but in the very few cases where this has not been possible our apologies are extended: pps 56, 58 (bottom), 59-60, © Avery Associates (photos Richard Holttum); pps 57-58, 61, photos Bryan Avery; pps 68-75, photos Dennis Gilbert; pps 76-81 photos © CCBG Architects; pps 88-95, 202, 204-7, photos © Christian Richters Fotograf; pps 106-107 (top), photos Graham Challifour; pg 107 (bottom), photos Fletcher Priest Architects; pps 108-109, photos Richard Davies; pg 110, photos Timothy Soar; pps 111-113, photos Chris Gascoigne; pg 120, photo Peter Mealin; pps 122-123, photos Nacasa & Partners; pps 124-130, 131-133, M Lorenzetti; pps 128-129, photos E Pfeiffer, pg 134, photo Benny Chan; pps158-165, © Shigeru Ohno (photos Atsushi Kitagawara); pg 167 © Maki and Associates; pps 170, 172 (top)-173 (top), photos Richard Johnson; pps 174, 176-177, photos Chris Henderson; pps 178-179, photos Paul Ratigan.

Cover: Dresden Cinema, Coop Himmelb(l)au
Frontispiece: AMC The Block 30, Orange, Jon Jerde
Page 6: Star City, Jon Jerde
Page 220: Pathe Cinema, Koen Van Velsen
Page 223: Dual 70/35mm Cinemeccanica professional cinematograph projection equipment
© Rank Organisation

First published in Great Britain in 2001 by
WILEY-ACADEMY

A division of
JOHN WILEY & SONS
Baffins Lane
Chichester
West Sussex PO19 1UD

ISBN: 0471491381

Other Wiley Editorial Offices
New York • Weinheim • Brisbane • Singapore • Toronto

Cover design: Artmedia Press, London
Series design: Artmedia Press, London
Typeset by Florence Production, Stoodleigh

Printed and bound in Italy

CONTENTS

PREFACE

The cinema is one of the newest building types. With only a little over a century of history, it has rapidly become ingrained in our consciousness as one of the indispensable places in our culture. It is also one of the few building types that is truly universal – cinemas are accessible to and enjoyed by almost everybody, regardless of class or culture. Unlike museums or theatres, cinemas are cultural centres which exclude no one. Each of us has a relationship with certain cinema buildings which are redolent with memories of dates and Saturday nights, of films that have engraved themselves on our minds and become part of our lives. Perhaps more than any other building, the cinema is a repository of nostalgia and of memories.

Often we feel nostalgia for cinemas that were never even part of our lives. When I see Odeons or Art Deco movie palaces, or if I see old cinema buildings abroad, I almost invariably find them intriguing. They seem to talk of a particular moment, of the huge importance attached to the movies – they express the critical status of film in modern life. I always feel a little depressed when I see these wonderful buildings boarded up or used as carpet warehouses, and even more depressed if I think of the neon-lit boxes on the edge of town, which have replaced them.

There are signs, however, that things are changing and that the importance of the movies in our cities is being realised. It would have been impossible to write this book only ten years ago, as there was too little of interest to cover. Over the last decade or so there has been an explosion in cinema architecture. That explosion has thrown out a few brilliant sparks and fragments but has also left a lot of ash and rubbish in its trail.

This selection can only be a very personal cross-section through the *oeuvre*. I have simply picked out the bits I like (and a few bits I don't like but think may be important) and discarded the rest. Even the history is only the most highly selective of romps. I have left out many of the greatest super-cinemas of the 1920s simply because they seem to me to be a poor extension of the architecture of the theatre and lacking in interest. On the other hand, I have dwelt on Art Deco and Expressionist cinemas because I feel that these buildings have repercussions which we are still feeling. The book is also a little weighted towards London; that is simply because I live here and grew up with some of its cinemas and am interested in how the newer buildings will take their place in the townscape.

Finally, I hope that everyone will find something here to inspire them or to give them faith that the future of the cinema is looking brighter than it has at any time since the periods we all look back upon in awe as the golden age.

Unknown Artist, Belgian Poster, c.1930

THE PICTURE HOUSE –
A NEW BUILDING TYPE

The roots of the picture house lie in travelling fairground booths and seedy, run-down dives; in rented halls, semi-derelict shops and dark, dangerous caverns with wooden benches. These darkened rooms were prone to burst into flame due to the notorious instability of early film materials and equipment. Within three decades of these unrespectable and inauspicious beginnings, the cinema had become the fastest growing and most recognisable new building type of the twentieth century. It became a new focus in the urban landscape – as influential as the church, and more so than the theatre or the vaudevillian music hall, which it replaced as the pivotal centre of public entertainment. In a staggeringly short space of time the cinema had become established as the undisputed everyman's venue for a night out.

Yet despite, or perhaps because of, its astonishingly rapid acceptance as a Saturday night institution, the cinema has always retained something of the brashness and the self-promoting vulgarity of the fairground booths of its origins. From the earliest peep shows, which attracted people with 'What the Butler Saw', to the vast out-of-town multiplexes showing Hollywood blockbusters on six screens, each steeped in the sickly sweet smell of popcorn and hot dogs, there remains a sense of the populist which seems both repellent and attractive. Like that other great new twentieth-century building type, the airport, the cinema promises new worlds, a transport to fantastic realms. It holds out the prospect of a new public forum – the cinema foyer, like the airport terminal, as a place for all classes and types to interact and communicate, a new urban hub. In fact, both the airport and the cinema tend towards the super-shed; sophisticated circulation systems with big hangars on the end, which fulfil the function of getting passengers or customers through the building as quickly and efficiently as possible, while spending plenty of money along the way.

However, between the early years of the fairground at the end of the nineteenth century and the years of the super-sheds in the late twentieth and early twenty-first centuries, there was an age when the cinema became a dream palace, a building which embodied escape and fantasy, a temporary relief from the mundane and repetitive world of work. Cinemas, every bit as much as films, are the physical embodiment of their eras. The extravagant choreographed musicals of Busby Berkeley and the glittering Art Deco picture palaces of the 1930s encapsulate the urge to escape from the depression and the insecurity which plagued the decade following the 1929 financial crash. The B-movie horror of aliens and radiation, and the drive-in theatres of the 1950s represented both the fear of Communism and the pioneering spirit of the USA with its self-mythologising love of freedom (the car) and the frontier spirit (open cinemas in the wilderness). The emergence of the art-house fleapit in the 1950s and 60s reflected a rebellion against Hollywood escapism and a belated response to Italian Neo-Realism (itself a response to the tragedy of the war). But it also denoted an acceptance of cinema as an avant-garde art form – the intellectuals wrenched glamour away from the cinema and replaced it with angst. The emergence of the super-cinemas, anonymous out-of-town complexes exclusively showing big studio blockbusters, echoed the *laissez-faire* and self-satisfaction of the Reagan/Thatcher era, an age of increasing corporate domination and decreasing acceptance of the avant-garde. The arrival of that even more overblown concept, the megaplex, coincided with the collapse of opposition to international capitalism, signalling the victory of corporate, global economics.

GRANADA WOOLWICH LONDON ENGLAND——THE MOST ROMANTIC THEATRE EVER BUILT

The popular roots of cinema initially agitated against its acceptance as an important art form. When film itself became recognised as the definitive twentieth-century art form, indeed the only truly popular modern art form, the cinemas were somehow left behind. As film was becoming credible, the Art Deco dream palaces were being destroyed. The frothy, shallow, tacked-on buildings that housed the defining years of film were never really regarded by the architectural establishment as part of their world. Cinemas were seen as every bit as ephemeral and disposable as the film sets that lit up their screens. In the 1930s, cinemas appeared in virtually every prosperous city, translating into built form the love of luxury that defined the decade, expressed in the detailing and streamlining of ocean liners and the glamour of Hollywood. With the incursions of television and, even more significantly, video in the 1970s and 80s, the cinemas were seen as redundant behemoths. Some were converted, many others demolished.

Perhaps no film better illustrates this demise than *Cinema Paradiso*, Giuseppe Tornatore's paean to the influence not just of film but of the physical fabric of the cinema. As the film's central character returns to his little town for the funeral of his beloved projectionist, the cinema is being torn down while a few old-timers who he remembers from his childhood look on sadly. The demolition of the cinema seems to indicate the destruction of community – it is being replaced by a car park – but also the abandonment of the communal dreams and fantasies which the cinema embodied.

Recently, however, the revival of city-centre cinemas and a few, lavish and enjoyably kitsch out-of-town monsterplexes has led to a revival of interest in the architecture of cinemas. In this book I hope to document the highlights of this revival and provide a cross-section of cinema building a century after its genesis.

FAIRGROUND TO DREAM PALACE – BUILDINGS FOR FILM

Films were first shown in existing buildings – sometimes rented halls, sometimes music halls or theatres which were temporarily converted, or sometimes, as news of the sensational new medium began to spread, in demountable fairground booths. When the cinema arrived as a new building type it took a form that can be seen as an amalgamation of elements from these existing buildings, combined with aspects of what could loosely be described as 'the architecture of entertainment'. By the architecture of entertainment I mean buildings erected for all kinds of picture shows which were the precursors of film, as well, of course, as theatres, which proved the most obvious precedent for the new building type.

Film was by no means the first answer to the desire to see moving images. It was preceded in the late eighteenth and nineteenth centuries by a plethora of techniques and machines capable of reproducing and projecting images to an excited audience. These techniques ranged from the intimacy of magic lanterns, which tended to be used in homes, to panoramas and dioramas, which were often housed in large, purpose-built structures. The camera obscura also became a popular form of entertainment in the nineteenth century, sometimes located in little pavilions, sometimes in domes above observatories or museums. Architecturally these buildings were often expressed as free-standing follies, an extension of the romantic garden architecture of the country house.

The diorama, a cylinder or globe which was painted and then animated using magic lanterns and lighting effects, demanded a larger, purpose-built structure and a few of these proved to be remarkable buildings, some modelled on the Pantheon, some featuring incredible globe structures which surrounded the visitor entirely in an event which was far more inclusive and embracing than cinema itself. A fine example of one of these

structures stood in London's Leicester Square in the middle of the nineteenth century and the section through the building illustrates a striking resemblance to Etienne-Louis Boullée's visionary design for a Cenotaph to Isaac Newton half a century earlier.

Other deliberately bizarre and mystical buildings were constructed as a blend of fairground hyperbole and architectural billboard. The Egyptian Hall in Piccadilly, erected in 1812 to show 'animated photographs', was one of the most spectacular examples. Its monumental self-advertisement, rich with stage-set historicism, became a paradigm for later cinema architects.

The origins of film lie in Thomas Edison's little box of tricks, the Kinetoscope, the first of which was produced in 1891. It was a mobile peep show, ideally suited to the coin-operated slot-machine culture of the itinerant fairgrounds. A single viewer peered into a viewing hole and, through a magnifying lens, saw a series of moving images. At the same time a number of other inventors were working on the idea of developing moving film into something which could be projected onto a screen, and the breakthrough was achieved by the Lumière brothers, who first screened their films to the public in Paris in 1895.

For the early years of their history, the Lumière brothers' *Cinématographe* and the machines of their competitors were used as sideshows. Film was a novelty and people went to see films because of their novelty value – the idea of narrative and story-telling through moving pictures developed a little later. Precisely because film was seen in this ephemeral light, many critics predicted that it would be a short-lived fad; as soon as people had grown weary of the novelty of moving pictures, cinema would go the way of other trends, like the diorama before it.

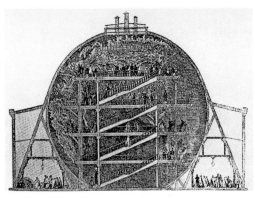

FROM TOP:
Camera Obscura, Victorian
Wylde's Great Globe, Leicester Square Gardens, 1851
Cross section through Wylde's Great Globe
Egyptian Hall, Piccadilly
Edison's Kinetoscope, 1891

Both Edison and the Lumière brothers, however, had extensive financial interests in film and its accompanying technology and it was in their interests to ensure that moving pictures proved to be more than a passing fashion. The development of narrative and of newsreels on film, and, the concept of movies could, rather cynically, be seen as a ruse to prolong the life of the technology, beyond the initial novelty. The critics' view of film as vulgar and artless was reinforced when moving pictures became a popular attraction at travelling fairgrounds. Short films were often accompanied by sideshows or vaudeville acts while showmen shouted for attention outside the travelling booths.

It was the fairgrounds, however, that were responsible for introducing cinema to the broader public, in the country and in provincial towns as well as in the great urban centres. Show people were instrumental in the evangelism of early motion pictures, sometimes even commissioning or producing films for which they would hold the exclusive rights. Although entrepreneurs had been quick to seize upon the potential of film by renting empty premises and halls and showing films, these were mostly slapdash affairs – films shown in unsuitable buildings and conditions by greedy businessmen trying to make a quick buck. The fairgrounds saw the genesis of purpose-built booths which, although demountable and often crowded, were in fact the first real cinemas.

In common with other fairground attractions, these booths, usually named bioscopes, were gaudy, fantastic affairs. Incredibly elaborate facades were erected to grab the attention of curious bystanders. These outrageously colourful, demountable fronts presaged the self-advertising facades of the movie theatres of the future, containing the origins of a billboard architecture that was to become the definitive approach to cinema building. It was precisely this commercial aesthetic which excluded cinemas from the avant-garde for much of the twentieth century. Architects who worked on cinemas were seen as mercenaries hanging onto the coat-tails of the voraciously commercial film companies.

This did not mean, however, that cinema designers disregarded the avant-garde and modern trends in architecture – quite the opposite in fact. Jean Desmet's 'Imperial Bio', which travelled around the Netherlands and Belgium during the first decade of the twentieth century, displayed a fantastically rich Art Nouveau facade. A style that was probably a little *passé* by the

LEFT: Imperial Bio, Jean Desmet
RIGHT: Limonaire Bioscope

time the booth was doing its rounds, it nevertheless encapsulated the radical nature of the new medium in its flowing curves and the inherent movement of the sinuous lines of the construction. The effects of Art Nouveau can equally be seen on the extravagant frontage of the Limonaire Bioscope of around 1907, where the whiplash lines of the *fin de siècle* are filled in with pudgy cherubs and more overtly and recognisably theatrical decoration.

It was soon realised that the device used to attract attention at the fairgrounds could equally effectively be applied to the converted halls and shop premises, which were beginning to dot every main street in the Western world in the first couple of decades of the twentieth century. A vividly coloured and heavily decorated facade could be added to an otherwise unspectacular building to create the illusion of luxury and of entering a new world of fantasy. Bright lights, gaudy posters, deep canopies and huge billboards were all adopted as symbols of the presence of the cinema on the street. Although the elements were refined into a formal architectural vocabulary, these remained the defining essence of cinema architecture for most of the ensuing century.

Cinemas are not complicated buildings. Essentially, early examples consisted of an auditorium, a box office and a projection booth plus a few ancillary facilities. Compared to the complex and often labyrinthine backstage requirements of a theatre building, which also demands a fly tower and complex stage machinery, the cinema is a relatively primitive affair. Early cinema buildings were generally more decorated versions of existing single-space buildings like billiard halls or social halls. A flashy facade featuring the cinema's name gave way to a barrel-vaulted or coffered-ceilinged auditorium with rich plaster decoration and panelled walls, perhaps with a small balcony. The extremely flammable nature of

early film stock led to frequent fires and subsequent regulations generally required the separation of the projection booth and different escape routes for audience and projectionist. The facades of these early buildings were clad in brightly coloured faience or terracotta, often with a large, arched opening, an arcade or a dome. The bigger cinemas which followed tended to be eclectic collections of Mannerist and Classical details in an often poorly defined cocktail.

The outbreak of the First World War in 1914 halted the development of the European cinema and saw America rise to sudden prominence. Before the war Germany had led the world in the development of a serious, modern cinema architecture. Oskar Kaufmann's 1911 Cines-Theatre in Berlin's Nollendorfplatz was one of the first significant free-standing purpose-built cinema structures. It was among the earliest attempts at a sober modern language of cinema architecture, presenting an austere picture to the world with three looming blank walls (perhaps an allusion to the simplicity and blankness of the screen). The subsequent development of Modernist cinema architecture is traced in another chapter and it was confined in its early years to northern Europe. America concentrated on the frivolous and the exotic. And how.

The luxury cinema or super-cinema arrived in the USA in the years directly before the First World War. Thomas W Lamb, a Scottish-born architect, designed the Regent in Harlem, New York, in 1913 and, in the next few years, he built a group of influential cinemas around Times Square – the Strand, the Rialto and the Rivoli – all in conjunction with the legendary impresario Samuel 'Roxy' Rothapfel. Together Lamb and Rothapfel defined the architecture of the luxury cinema and created the notion of the picture palace as a place of escape and sheer fantasy in which the building played as large a part in an evening out as the film itself.

These cinemas were impressive Classical buildings, some with touches of Venetian, Gothic and Baroque or of English country house. This eclectic travel through European history culminated in 1927 with the Roxy, Rothapfel's shrine to his own vision. Seating nearly 6,000, it was truly a dream palace, executed in a Mediterranean Renaissance jumble of Spanish and Portuguese motifs, its interior doused in gold. It looked like the Beverley Hills mansion of a newly rich movie star. Teetering on the verge of hideous, it was not tasteful but it was built to impress. The Roxy's architect, Walter Ahlschlager, managed to fit a capacious, fan-shaped auditorium onto an awkward, L-shaped site entered via a sensuously oval foyer. The cinema's demolition hardly more than thirty years later was to prove a poignant moment as it not only indicated the end of the dream and success of the movie palace in a mere generation, but also sparked off the notion of cinema as heritage among a few enthusiasts, ultimately leading to the conservation and listing of cinema buildings and their preservation as landmarks.

The super-cinemas outside the USA tended to be more restrained. The huge Plaza in Regent Street, London (1926), showed the refinement of its architect, Frank Verity, who was associated with the West End theatres. The same architect's earlier Pavilion in Shepherd's Bush (1923) was an attempt to give the cinema an imperial Roman grandeur by imitating the brick arches and monumental forms of Diocletian's Baths. To infuse a London cinema with some Hollywood glamour, Thomas W Lamb was imported to design the Empire, Leicester Square in 1928. The result was a luxurious interior but a facade that seemed to have developed little from the earliest cinema buildings, with a kind of triumphal arch effect.

The Roxy, however, remained unsurpassable in its magnificence and luxury. As it could not be matched in terms of gilt and mouldings, architects had to look down other avenues to create new cinemas which would compete with the glamour of the Roxy. They looked everywhere, from China to Ancient Egypt, from Mediterranean villages to the Art Deco style which wafted the scent of French elegance and sophistication, of wealth and skyscrapers, and of the big city.

TOP and MIDDLE: Audrocium of The Roxy, New York, 1927
BOTTOM: Plaza, Regent Street, London, 1926

THE EXOTIC AND THE ATMOSPHERIC

As movies began to replace vaudeville and music hall as the essential, accessible entertainment for the masses, theatres began to be invaded by projection booths, which grew parasitically at the back of the host auditoria as live entertainment gave way to screens. As longer films with narratives became popular around the period of the First World War, the blend of live entertainment and short films, which had been seen as necessary to attract crowds, became obsolete, and films began to be seen as viable entertainment on their own. D W Griffith's *Birth of a Nation* (1915) proved a massive hit and, at over three hours long, finally proved that cinema could provide epic entertainment to match the theatre and stand on its own both as an art form and as an evening out.

A crucial part of the experience of the popular theatre had traditionally been to afford a level of luxury to which audiences were not accustomed. The theatre provided an escape from the dullness of everyday life in cramped apartments and boring, repetitive jobs. Early cinema promoters took this idea of escapist fantasy to heart and decided to outdo the theatres. Film could transport the viewer to exotic locations and glamorous places in a way that theatrical directors could only dream of doing. Whole new experiences opened up as audiences could travel through the screen in an almost mythical process. Whereas theatre builders had attempted to imbue their buildings with the cultural symbols of the Rococo and the Beaux Arts – traditions which were seen to lend weight to their status as successors of the Italian opera and the European royal theatres – cinema builders realised that they were bound by no such cultural constraints.

The first cinema buildings were inevitably influenced by the language of the theatre as the closest existing building type; boxes, balconies and stages all made

their appearances. But to reinforce the exoticism and the romantic fantasies that were the main selling point of film, entrepreneurs began introducing fantastic buildings to give a flavour of the wonders that could be beheld within. The cinema building became a physical trailer for the main attraction of the film itself.

The USA had become rich from the First World War but its citizens were deprived of one of their major sources of entertainment and social life – alcohol. At the same time the millions of immigrants arriving from Europe had little command of English, rendering theatre irrelevant to them. Silent film stepped in with a language of slapstick and *Grand Guignol*. It became a universal medium that could talk to foreigners and illiterates alike. Immigrants who had fled to America (and in Europe had fled the country for the cities) in search of streets paved with gold, found the next best thing: auditoria of gold and velvet in the outrageously elaborate cinemas – palaces of exoticism which made them feel that they too could temporarily immerse themselves in the dream of luxury. This kind of extravagant, exotic auditorium became one of the fastest growing genres and was the first move away from European historicist styles. It could be argued that this kitsch, stagy and escapist architecture constituted the first coherent built expression of the movie theatre and the first architectural approach to cinema design that can be defined as a recognisable style.

One of the finest examples of the architectural exoticism which gripped cinema builders in the 1920s is Grauman's (now Mann's) Chinese Theater. The tall, pagoda-style copper roof, red lacquer doors and the pillars of the forecourt (which Grauman is said to have imported from a Chinese palace) have become key symbols of Hollywood. In an industry notorious for discarding the out of fashion, the Chinese Theater is a remarkably durable survivor which has been given an

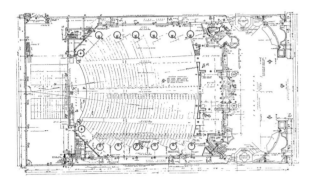

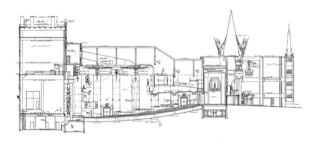

TOP and MIDDLE: Grauman's Chinese Theater, Hollywood, 1922,
Plan and Section
BOTTOM: Egyptian Man, Piccadilly, 1812

extended lease of life by the presence of the 'Pavement of the Stars'.

Sid Grauman, builder of the Chinese Theater, was a remarkable showman and a pioneer of the exotic cinema. His first fantasy venue was erected near the site of the Chinese Theater on Hollywood Boulevard in 1922. The screen of Grauman's Egyptian was framed by four huge, fat Ancient Egyptian-style columns, crowned with papyrus-reed capitals, their shafts adorned with hieroglyphics. The auditorium was awash with golden decoration and pictographs, with an incredibly rich ceiling and a host of scarabs and sphinxes. The building was designed by Meyer and Holler who would work on the Chinese Theater five years later.

The Egyptian Theater was opened in the same year that Howard Carter discovered the tomb of Tutankhamen. It is a phenomenal testament to the power of Carter's discovery and its effect on popular culture. Many of the Ancient Egyptian motifs would form the basis of the Art Deco style that emerged over the following few years. But the Egyptian is also an interesting example of how fashions are revived: the Egyptian Hall in Piccadilly was a staggering building in the heart of London which had been showing displays of 'animated photographs' (next to a museum of Egyptian artefacts) over a century before Grauman's cinematic fantasy was conceived. The style quickly took root in Paris too, where Ripey built the Louxor Pathé in 1921, while in London its later incarnation is superbly represented by the sculptural, polychromatic frontage of George Coles' 1930 Carlton in the Essex Road.

However, the golden age of exotic theatres was dominated by orientalism. Interestingly, just as the Egyptian picture house was presaged by earlier designs in England, the orientalism which became the staple of exoticism in the USA of the 1920s was not a purely American innovation (or aberration as the later Modernists were to see it), as many architectural histories have suggested.

Oskar Kaufmann's 1911 Cines-Theatre in Berlin's Nollendorfplatz has already been mentioned as one of the first cinemas to develop a modern architectural language. But despite its general austerity, its main elevation featured a half-domed recessed entrance which was crowned by a huge 'Buddha-like' statue. The Buddha subsequently appeared in a number of luxuriously appointed American theatres, including Loew's extravagant 72nd Street Picture Theater. R C Reamer's Fifth Avenue Theater in Seattle, Washington

(1926), smothered its audience in a treasure chest of chinoiserie, including reproductions of motifs from the Forbidden Palace in Beijing.

Architects followed trends on the screen. There was a rash of movies with exotic and oriental themes, from D W Griffith's *Broken Blossoms* (1919) to Fritz Lang's *The Spiders* and *Hara-kiri* (both also 1919). Their themes were reflected in cinema interiors dripping with golden ornament, intricate pierced screens and complex composite columns, every surface studded with carvings and mouldings. These dream-like temple interiors were both absurd and striking, precursors to the childish awe which theme parks attempt to instil by taking visitors around the world (or the world of movies) in a brief, self-contained visit.

Islamic imagery also proved a staple influence on early cinema architects. The very name 'Alhambra' conjures up half-remembered fleapits. Rapp and Rapp's Oriental Theater in Chicago (1925) was the classic of its type and curry-house domes and ogee windows followed throughout the world. Again, early developments in England had presaged this trend. The Electric Theatre in Praed Street, London, and The Globe in Putney (both 1910) were originally resplendent in ill-fitting Mughal costumes. It took Valentino in *The Sheik* (1921) and *Blood and Sand* (1922) to make cinema builders realise the full exotic potential of Islamic imagery. But when women fainted *en masse* at these pictures, movie architectures own version of Victorian Orientalist art burst forth.

The frenetic search for new forms and the competition of the exotic era led US architects to look at America's indigenous architecture, in particular the pyramids and temples of Central America. Inspired at least partly by Frank Lloyd Wright's intricately detailed houses of the early 1920s, American architects embarked on an encounter with their forebears. The arrival of concrete as a building material gave rise to massive temples to the cinema fabricated from pre-cast elements, a type of construction which lent itself easily to the casting of Mayan motifs into concrete panels. Morgan, Walls and Clements' Mayan Theater in Los Angeles (1922) was a spectacularly theatrical tribute to that ancient civilisation, replete with paintings and sculptures. The style even reached the other side of the Pacific with Walter Burley Griffin's Capital Theatre in Melbourne (1924). This kind of design was later subsumed into the broader Art Deco genre. It was superceded by another effort at an architectural language for the cinema – the colonial style. Well

FROM TOP: Grauman's Egyptian Theater, LA, 1922
Carlton, Islington, 1930
Mayan Theater, LA, 1922

Capital Theater, Chicago, 1926, a typical Eberson atmospheric

Astoria, Brixton, 1929, British atmospheric

suited to the heat of California, this architecture mirrored the garish neo-colonial houses of Beverley Hills with a blend of Spanish and vernacular details. Morgan, Walls and Clements were the first to master this style too. Their Music Box and Belasco theatres of the early 1920s, both in Hollywood, were the best examples.

Once the architectures of aristocratic Europe, the rest of the world and then even Pre-Columbian America and all the other defunct civilisations which had been plundered, the next step was the idealised Mediterranean village. In an act of rebellion against the gold and plush velvet of classical theatre architecture and the heavy trappings of architectural exoticism, a group of architects began a kind of exodus to Southern European shores. Like writers retreating to Provence or Tuscany to find peace in an idealised landscape of tranquil eternity, the architects turned from the exotic to the quaintly atmospheric. In fact that is how this new style came to be known. The atmospheric theatre aimed to give the impression of a Mediterranean evening al fresco. Little white houses with pan-tiled roofs looked down upon the audience, ivy and vines trailing from their walls. It was the increasingly complex art of the production designer feeding back into the space on this side of the screen.

The undisputed champion of the atmospheric interior was an immigrant who had studied architecture in Vienna and arrived in the USA in 1901, John Eberson. A magnificent self-publicist, Eberson was one of the most prolific and influential cinema designers the world has seen. His European training and facility with Beaux Arts forms gave him a respectability and standing amongst both patrons and critics. The essence of Eberson's work was a fantasy auditorium which evoked a European or otherwise romantic open-air setting. The internal walls were built to resemble the facades of

Moorish palaces or Italian piazzi with an abundance of wherefore-art-thou-Romeo balconies and quaint tiled roofs. Cypress trees, arcades and fountains at every corner reinforced the effect, while the single, smooth, all-enveloping surfaces of the great vaulted ceilings were painted to resemble the sky. It could almost be seen as a paean to the Classical Greek theatre, set against a landscape revered in pantheistic terms and overlooked by the gods. It was not irrelevant to the wildfire spread of these atmospheric theatres that they were cheaper to construct because there was no need for lavishly decorated ceilings with rich plasterwork and gilded ornaments; just a simple, painted sky.

A more prosaic, but probably more useful analogy than the Classical theatres of Greece would be the early cinemas, known as air-domes, which proliferated in the USA in the first years of film. These were structures open to the sky but contained by four walls. The absence of a roof reduced the risks from fire in the days of nitrate film and sparking projectors and also eliminated the need for expensive ventilation schemes. This idea of the open sky must have seemed attractive enough to reinstate as an architectural reference. Indeed many of the most elaborate atmospheric theatres boasted lighting effects and decoration to create 'manufactured weather'. Eberson himself described the ideas behind the designs: 'We visualise and dream … a magnificent amphitheatre under a glorious moonlit sky in an Italian garden, in a Persian court, in a Spanish patio, or in a mystic Egyptian temple-yard, all canopied by a soft moonlit sky.' Eberson also summed up his approach in the more mercenary alliterative maxim: 'Prepare Practical Plans for Pretty Playhouses – Please Patrons – Pay Profits.' (Both quotes taken from Sharp, Dennis, *The Picture Palace*, London, Hugh Evelyn, 1969, pp 74–76.)

From the 1920s onwards, Eberson was responsible

Astoria, Brixton, 1920

Granada, Woolwich, 1937

for over a hundred of these atmospheric theatres all over the USA. Europe proved less susceptible to these fantasy palaces, but by the early 1930s a number of extravagantly exotic picture palaces did begin to appear. The master of the exotic interior in England was a Russian *émigré*, Theodore Komisarjevsky. He was not an architect; his background was in stage design and his work on cinemas was on their interiors alone. Through the 1930s Komisarjevsky's work, particularly on the Granada chain of cinemas, was a consistent stream of lavish fantasy settings, starting with Moorish-style designs based on the Alhambra, and moving on to blends of Gothic, Venetian, Byzantine and Rococo stylings. These themed interiors were often contained within architect-designed structures that were incongruously Moderne, using motifs from Modernism, Art Deco and expressionistic streamlining in commercial settings in a sort of diluted version of the avant-garde. In a way, this curious disjunction of modernistic facades and the lavish, gilt halls within became a kind of successful evocation of moving to the interior of the cinema, to be transported to another realm, a world of fantasy and delight, making the transition and the curious juxtaposition of styles less jarring than might appear to be the case. The Granada in Tooting, London, (1931) is a fine example of this surreal juxtaposition of Moderne with Venetian Gothic. It was described as a 'Doge's Palace' for South London.

These atmospheric and exotic theatres in both the USA and Britain coexisted side by side with the emergent streamlined Moderne cinemas but gradually their convoluted surfaces and gilded details began to look *outré* as first Art Deco and then Modernism stamped themselves on the public consciousness. The early Deco cinemas were every bit as fantastic and theatrically decorative as the exotic excesses but their

jazzy Modernism referred to the new age of Hollywood rather than to the historicist vocabulary so beloved by Amerson, Komisarjevsky et al.

It is tempting to say that the exotic and atmospheric theatre represented the last burst of historicism in cinema architecture, that after the decline of the style, Art Deco, Moderne and Modernism took over. But, although convenient, it would be a gross oversimplification. Komisarjevsky's stunning interpretation of the Gothic became increasingly theatrical as the 1930s progressed and as late as 1937 he decorated the interior of the Granada at Woolwich, London with a bizarre mix of Romanesque and cathedral Gothic. The interior created a kind of shocking double-take within a streamlined shell by Cecil Masey, a building that blended Northern European Modernist and Expressionist motifs in its smoothly curving frontage, with elements of Art Deco. In fact this building is a typical late example of an important transitional phase which began in the years around 1930 when Art Deco, Modernism, Expressionism and all kinds of theatrical historicist applied styles coexisted for a brief period.

Whether simply for economic reasons, for practical and acoustic reasons or for reasons of fashion, the 1930s saw the last gasp of the atmospheric theatre as Art Deco and Moderne gradually became *de rigueur*. The Art Deco dream palaces of the 1930s took over as the pinnacle of cinematic design, just as historical epics went out of fashion on screen to be replaced by the mass choreography of the new musicals which took advantage of the arrival of sound on film. It would be Busby Berkeley rather than D W Griffith or Cecil B de Mille who would influence the look of the front of house as much as they would the movies themselves.

ART DECO – DREAM PALACES TO STREAMLINED PALACES

Art Deco is the style more associated with cinemas than any other and it is worth looking at separately as a remarkable international phenomenon. The greatest boom in cinema building more or less coincided with the lifespan of Art Deco. The cinemas of the early twentieth century tended to be placed in existing buildings which were converted, or in purpose-built structures which imitated the forms and conventions of the theatre. When cinema building really began to take off in the early 1920s, a panoply of historicist styles dominated architecture and cinemas were effectively dressed up in historical costume. In Europe a sombre conservatism dominated the years which came in the shadow of the First World War, while in the USA cinema architects tended to work in an optimistic vaudevillian style which, although often attractive, varied widely in appearance, solidity and skill. The arrival of Art Deco in the mid-1920s spawned an architectural approach that would become synonymous with cinema design. It became the first – and in fact the only – universally recognised building style for cinemas. The reasons for this spectacular success are varied, stemming from the genesis of the new style.

Art Deco effectively grew out of Art Nouveau. As the organic motifs of the *fin de siècle* became abstracted into geometric motifs by designers and architects, particularly Charles Rennie Mackintosh in Glasgow and Josef Hoffmann in Vienna, Art Nouveau began to mutate into proto-Art Deco. Art Nouveau had some effect on cinema design. It proved a relatively easy way of sticking new-looking, highly dramatic decoration on an existing building without incurring too much cost. Whiplash lines and organic tendrils appeared on a number of cinema fronts, as, for example, on Jean Desmet's temporary bioscope building or the over-the-top, tarted-up facade of the Queriol in Lisbon (1907).

One building in particular bridged the gap between the end of Art Nouveau and Secessionism and the beginnings of Art Deco – Henri Louis de Jong's remarkable Tuschinski in Amsterdam (1918-21). Clad in exotically moulded faience and blending Art Nouveau and Expressionist details, this odd but strikingly powerful cinema with its twin cupolas and elephants' heads foreshadowed the decorative excesses and exuberance of early Art Deco as early as 1918. The Tuschinski, however, was an anomaly which can be related perhaps more to the development of the Expressionism of the Amsterdam school than to the emergence of Art Deco.

The First World War interrupted the development of the growing obsession with geometric forms but the fascination with intricate abstract decoration began to re-emerge in the 1920s, particularly in Paris. Until then this approach had been largely limited to the applied arts, but in 1925 Paris hosted the Exposition Internationale des Arts Decoratifs et Industriels Modernes, and the temporary pavilions erected for this fair proved to be the perfect opportunity for designers to apply these decorative techniques to architecture as well as to *objets d'art*. The exuberantly decorative panache of Art Deco was an antidote to post-war depression and filled the gap which had existed in architecture for a popular new style. Art Deco seemed to exude optimism and confidence and to embody Parisian elegance and fashion. In fact before the exposition its only manifestations in architecture were in jewellery stores and boutiques – it became a kind of aspirational style. The only other option for architects who were trying to express the new spirit was Modernism. Two of the most brilliant exponents of radical Modernism built pavilions at the 1925 Expo – Le Corbusier and Konstantin Melnikov. Their stark buildings for *L'Esprit Nouveau* and the Soviet Union respectively, were pushed to the sides of the Expo where they wouldn't shame those who had expended a proper amount of energy on decorating their structures.

From this Parisian Exposition, Art Deco took off on a fantastic scale. It became the architecture which defined the early years of new building types: skyscrapers, the new breed of super-hotels, even ocean-liners and, perhaps most importantly, cinemas. One of the reasons that Art Deco proved so popular with cinema architects was its simplicity. There is really no such thing as Art Deco architecture; it is merely a decorative style, a series of familiar motifs which are applied to a building. This allowed architects to carry on building movie theatres in their accustomed way and dress them up with swish details which would make the building instantly recognisable as new, as fashionable and as a cinema.

Another significant factor was the initial association with Paris, capital of style and elegance, and subsequently with the USA, where Art Deco became synonymous with the American building boom of the 1920s and with the golden era of the movies and the on-screen lives of the rich and spoilt. With these combined associations, Art Deco became a stylistic cipher for luxury and wealth for cinema owners who wanted to create an impression of splendour and escapism to audiences who hankered after a glimpse of the American dream. Theatre architects in *fin de siècle* London had turned to French Rococo and Louis XIV and XVI designs in an attempt to create the impression of fantastic luxury and elegance, attainable (for the price of a mere ticket) by the masses. The cinema builders turned to the same associations of glamour and riches which attached themselves to the Deco style.

In the mid-1920s Art Deco appeared as one option for cinema architects, a style amongst many others to choose from. In fact it developed quite seamlessly from the kind of monumental, stripped Classicism which had begun to appear in cinemas. The Kensington Cinema (now Odeon) in London, designed by Leathart and Grainger in 1927, is a fine example of the kind of solidly built super-cinema that teeters on the edge of three styles – Monumental Classical, Art Deco and Modernist. Blocky and pared down, the building is given expressiveness by its considered massing, the insertion of black polished stone against the white ashlar, and its geometric composition. A couple of years later Leathart and Grainger built the Richmond Cinema which takes this embryonic Deco Classicism a stage closer to full-blown Deco, although the

FROM TOP: Tuschinski, Amsterdam, 1918–21
Art deco panels, New Victoria, London,
romance and thriller

ABOVE: Cartoon from Punch, 1933
BELOW: Odeon, Kensington, 1927

architects, probably unwillingly, inserted an incongruous atmospheric interior into this pared-down shell. It was only a short step to the classic Deco of the same firm's Sheen Cinema of 1930 (now demolished), which uses the same symmetrical blockiness to bring an elegant solidity to suburban London.

This kind of stripped Classical monumentality (which also later became the de facto architecture of Fascism, Stalinism and all the other governments of the pre-war era, including, notably, the Roosevelt administration) became associated with the rise of the super-cinemas. These huge buildings, which were erected throughout Europe and the USA, heralded the true arrival and dominance of cinema as the main attraction. Around 1930, Deco emerged as the victor in the battle for the style of the cinema. Soon it had become more or less *de rigueur*. This fantastic dominance saw the architecture of the Art Deco movie palace shift into a second phase.

The greatest of the Art Deco cinemas of the late 1920s tended to be fantastic, palatial buildings in which huge audiences could immerse themselves in the Hollywood dream. The dazzling, metallic splendour of S Charles Lee's Wiltern Theater (1929-31) and B Marcus Priteca's Pantages Theater (1929-30), both in Los Angeles, described the peak of Art Deco as applied ornamentation. Both cinemas were essentially theatres in form, even down to the proscenium arch and stages. Opulently decorated, no surface was left without gilded abstract reliefs, while fantastical, crystalline light fittings hung from the centres of the ceilings. Lee's Fox Theater in Phoenix, Arizona (1931), his Fox Wilshire, Beverley Hills, California (1928-30) and Miller and Pflueger's Paramount Theater in Oakland, California are all superb examples of the high Art Deco style which proliferated all over the USA during this period. The style was also adopted enthusiastically (if briefly) in Europe; Marcel Chabot's 1931 Cinema Eldorado in Brussels and Georges Gumpel's Théâtre de l'Alhambra of 1927 are both fine European manifestations of high Deco. The gushing neon fountain which surmounted the ziggurat roof of Henri Belloc's Gaumont, Paris, was one of European Art Deco's most spectacular sights.

These cinemas represent both the peak of the Art Deco architecture which arose from the Paris Exposition, but also the end of an era. Two changes were to transform radically the nature of cinema architecture at the end of the 1920s, and Art Deco would move into a second phase. The first of these changes occurred in 1927 – the arrival of the talkies. The reason that the introduction of sound into the movies had such a profound effect was that all those details – the boxes and drapes, the grilles and sculptural reliefs – absorbed sound and made for poor acoustics in the auditoria. This would eventually lead to the adoption of cleaner lines, smoother surfaces and a faux-aerodynamic style which became known as streamlining. The second factor which helped architects on their way to streamlining buildings occurred two years after *The Jazz Singer* introduced audiences to the talkies – the Wall Street Crash of 1929. The golden sculptures and aluminium sunbursts that defined the Art Deco of the late 1920s not only gave the impression of luxury, but by the depressed 1930s became seen as a luxury. Although the lavish downtown theatres remained an attraction, people with less money in their pockets were less able to afford such opulence. They tended to stay in the suburbs and make do with modest local attractions. This trend led to the consolidation of the second phase of Art Deco, the phenomenal spread of the style to the local cinema.

Art Deco coexisted with the Modern Movement, even though it was looked down on as populist and as no better than a historicist style by the purists who drove the development of the International Style. However, the practitioners of Art Deco and the builders of the cinema boom of the 1920s and 30s were often influenced by the work of the pioneer Modernists who denigrated them. The diluted, streamlined Modernism that defined the new wave of 1930s cinemas was most people's first encounter with modern architecture. This was particularly true in Britain where Modernism was slow to take off. So despite the contempt in which this kind of commercial and blatantly populist architecture was held by the avant-garde, it played an important role in introducing the reductivist principles of modern architecture to the masses. It is also easy to take the cynical view and comment that the stripped-down aesthetics of streamlining coincided neatly with the Depression and a severe drop in profit margins: exotic cinemas and lavishly decorated and gilded Art Deco movie palaces became too expensive to maintain, let alone to build.

The early twentieth century saw radical changes in the design of conventional theatres – the elaborate Francophile auditoria, bursting with gilded *putti* and cartouches, fell out of favour as the pioneers of realism and subsequently Modernism in drama demanded that attention be focused on the stage not on the surroundings. The changes in the design of cinema auditoria during the early 1930s were driven by

FROM TOP: Fox Theater, Phoenix, Arizona
A typical lavish deco auditorium streamlining appears on the stairs and bar, Hippodrome, Coventry, 1937

commercial rather than artistic criteria but the end result was similar; the attention was increasingly focused on the screen rather than the splendour of the architecture. Streamlining proved amenable to this directionality because the horizontal, banded emphasis derived from ideas of speed and movement in the design of locomotives, cars, ships and aeroplanes helped to direct the eye ineluctably towards the screen. Cinema architects began to shift slightly from the conventional theatrical model of an auditorium and the 1930s saw the plans of cinemas developing into a shape derived from projection and sight lines for screen rather than stage. It was during this period that the familiar fan-shaped auditorium began to appear in cinema buildings. This shape itself can be seen as a kind of streamlining of the plan, signalling a functionalist modern approach which had hitherto remained almost entirely alien to mainstream cinema architects.

As the 1930s progressed, the extravagant detailing and mouldings which defined early Art Deco architecture became ever more refined and abstracted until only a few expressionistic lines and curves remained (rather like the few simple pen-strokes which animators add to a drawing to indicate a character that has just departed in a whoosh of speed).

This late Art Deco architecture, streamlined, sculptural and abstracted, also lent itself well to the increasing suburbanisation of the USA and Western Europe. Cinema facades were extruded into bold, sculptural masses which could not fail to draw attention to themselves in the low-rise suburban landscape. Movie theatres became symbols. Always recognisable, brilliantly illuminated at night and standing out boldly against the sky when seen from the road during the day, the cinema building itself became a giant billboard. The position of the streamlined late Deco movie theatre in the development of the archetypal cinema has recently been confirmed by Cesar Pelli's new building for Walt Disney's idealised American small-town, 'Celebration'. Pelli's cinema is a straight pastiche of a late 1930s movie theatre.

The archetypal 1930s cinema became perhaps the most recognisable manifestation of the movie house as the heart of the community. Recent moves towards awareness of the importance of these buildings in the townscape in Europe as well as in the USA have brought them out of the obscurity in which they languished in the post-war years. They have played a pivotal role in defining the popular image of what a cinema should look like.

Hippodrome, Coventry, 1937

MODERNISM AND THE CINEMA

The development of the cinema as a new building type and the history of Modernism occurred virtually simultaneously. Just as the foundations of Modernist architecture were being laid at the end of the nineteenth and the beginning of the twentieth centuries, so cinemas began to move from the fairground to the city centre. This concurrence of a new type of architecture and a new type of building would, it might be assumed, have led to cinema designers being at the forefront of the Modern Movement. Architects could demonstrate their new ideas in genuinely popular new buildings which incorporated the new technologies which so fascinated Modernists, all in the urban centres which were the heartlands of this new revolution. But this was not the case at all. Film quickly became the most popular of all artistic media and, in two important respects, this conspired against the coming together of Modernism and cinema building.

The first reason was the populism of the film distributors and theatre owners. Modernism was by no means a popular style until, perhaps, the era after the Second World War, and the builders of theatres wanted, above all, supremely popular cinemas which would appeal to as wide an audience as possible. Thus, they aspired first to the models of the atmospheric and exotic cinemas and later to the Hollywood glamour and spangle of Art Deco. The second reason can be summed up as a snobbishness emanating from the Modernists themselves. The cinema was looked down upon by the pioneers of Modernism who were often happy to experiment with theatres and their intellectual audiences but were far less happy when confronted with the idea of a popular cinema. The supreme irony here is that the Socialist ideals that lay at the heart of European Modernism were disregarded utterly when architects and theoreticians were confronted with a type of building that the urban proletariat may have actually enjoyed using.

Modernism and cinema architecture were not, however, entirely mutually exclusive. A few architects managed to buck the trend and create buildings that achieved the rare status of blending the avant-garde and the popular. Among the most important of these architects was the Modernist pioneer Theo van Doesburg. L'Aubette (1926-28) in Strasbourg, an institution incorporating a cinema that must have been similar to a modern arts centre, was an intervention into the existing fabric of an eighteenth-century building. Van Doesburg was in charge of the project but he appointed other leading artistic figures to design separate components of the scheme. The building became one of the finest examples of the *Gesamtkunstwerk*, or the total work of art, to come to fruition in the early years of Modernism. Van Doesburg's design encompassed the large and the small-scale, from the signage to the crockery for the cafés. The interiors were one of the most important

L'Aubette, Strasbourg, 1926–28

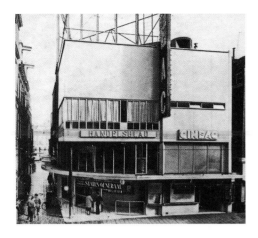

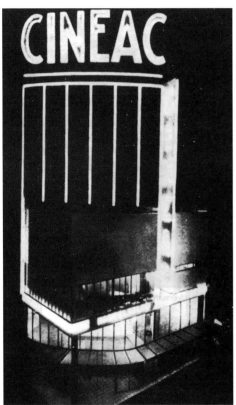

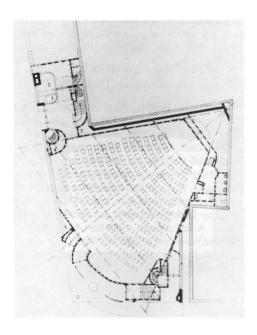

Cineac, Amsterdam, 1934
FROM TOP: Daytime, night-time, plan

realisations of De Stijl and were heavily influenced by Russian Constructivism. Van Doesburg's idea was that the building should be perceived like a De Stijl painting and that it would be possible to live within the canvas of this three-dimensional picture. The familiar primary colours and bold rectangular geometries of Mondrian and Rietveld were built up in three dimensions to create a set of fascinating (although cold) interiors. Virtually the swansong of De Stijl architecture, L'Aubette was an important work in art historical terms but a complete flop with the public and it was altered and changed almost beyond recognition within a few years of opening.

Along with L'Aubette, the design of another Dutchman has become one of the most iconic Modernist cinemas, the Cineac in Amsterdam. Johannes Duiker's 1934 building is squeezed onto a tight site in central Amsterdam and its corner is cut away at street level to create an entrance canopy out of the overhanging structure above. Using a severely reductivist architectural vocabulary, Duiker succeeded in blurring the interior and exterior worlds of activity with extensive floor-to-ceiling glazing. Elsewhere the walls consist of plain, unadulterated Modernist whiteness. In contrast to this purity, Duiker seems to have taken an almost post-Venturi delight in the vast signage that emerges from the roof on enormous stilts, following the line of the cut-away corner and continuing down the street facade, dominating the building. This combines with the illumination emanating from the expansive glazing of the elevations, so that the Cineac sparkles at night. The almost grotesquely overdone lighting and signage announce that this is a building about the projection of lights and images and that its interior is a continuation of the public realm.

The interior is equally original and narrows towards the screen to form a curious ovoid shape (seen on ground-floor plan as a delta shape), which embraces the whole audience, much as the traditional horseshoe shape of European opera houses enfolded the audience while focusing attention on the stage. The Cineac is located opposite the Tuschinski and its stripped, machine aesthetic is intended as an obvious affront to the Expressionist decoration of the earlier building – if the Tuschinski is a palace of dreams and escapism, Duiker is determined to show the Cineac, a news cinema, as a place of engagement with the city and with the real world. The building has fared better than Van Doesburg's unfortunate masterpiece and remains a strikingly modern presence in the Amsterdam streetscape.

Duiker's Cineac blends two traditions: the stripped language of Modernism with an almost agitprop lettering at least partly derived from the Constructivist tradition of the Soviet revolutionary period. This screaming neon lettering may look more reminiscent of Las Vegas than Moscow, but Duiker's precedents would have been the political rather than the commercial realm of graphic design – although this example shows quite how close these two aspects of cinema design actually were. The building itself, however, is firmly rooted in a tradition of Modernism in cinema design which can be traced back, at least as far as Erik Gunnar Asplund's exquisitely understated Skandia Cinema in Stockholm (1922-23).

This building consists of a stripped Classical auditorium, reduced to the bare elements, and a well-planned and rational series of circulation spaces which remove all pretension from the idea of theatricality. The long, densely packed rectangle of the auditorium (with galleries all around in a shape reminiscent of the inn-type theatres of Shakespearean England) is one of the most pleasing of early cinemas. Little is allowed to distract the audience from the screen. The eccentric detailing of the entrances to the auditorium, each with a curious combination of Nordic Classical detailing, is a real oddity and seems to presage the Post-Modernist work of Aldo Rossi among others. The delicate Classical details and fine proportions of the fittings also illustrate the closeness of Classicism to Modernism.

The Skandia itself is part of a line which can be traced back even further to the nearby Roda Kvarn in the same city, designed by Edvard Bernhard between 1915 and 1917. Bernhard's cinema is also an exemplar of the kind of straightforward, pared-down Northern Classicism which foreshadowed the Modern Movement. Only a few strips of lightbulbs on the otherwise black facade offer any clue to the nature of the entertainment within.

At exactly the same time as the Roda Kvarn was being built, another architect experimented with a blend of Classical proportions and modern architectural language in a manner that foreshadowed some of Asplund's work. Le Corbusier's Cinema La Scala is a building that sits on the brink of Modernism. Built in 1916 in La Chaux-de-Fonds in Switzerland, La Scala was virtually the last of Le Corbusier's buildings to use the Classical architectural language. Widely criticised and denigrated at the time, this odd, temple-fronted

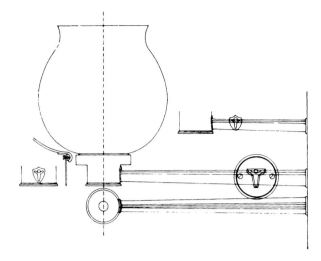

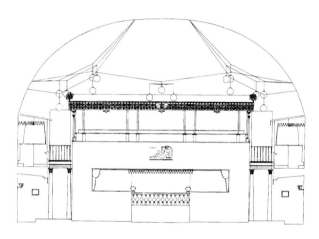

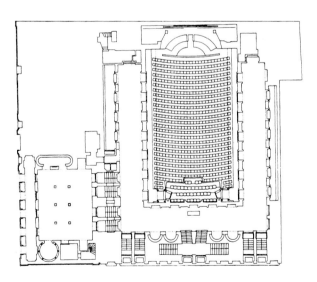

Skandia Cinema, Stockholm, 1922–23
FROM TOP: Light detail, cross section, plan

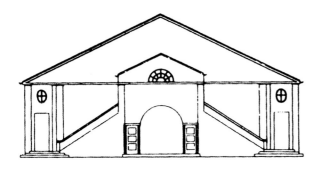

TOP: La Scala, LA Chaux-De Fonds, 1916
BOTTOM: Design for a screen-tribute-kiosk, G. Klutsis, 1922

structure stands like the underscaled work of some French Revolutionary architect, a doll's-house version of Boullée's visionary monuments. A building that doesn't quite fit in with the Modernist view of the development of architecture, this eccentric little structure is often left out of conventional histories and Corb biographies but remains important nevertheless.

At around the same time as Asplund was developing and refining his Neo-Classical-Modern version of cinema architecture at the Skandia, a group of architects in Russia were designing vehicles for film as political propaganda to proselytise the virtues of the Bolshevik revolution to the masses. Film was used (employing the country's best directors) as a political and revolutionary medium, shown in a variety of converted premises, trains and mobile cinemas. The temporary architecture of these structures and vehicles was executed in the language of agitprop. Cheaply constructed yet visually stunning, they exerted an impact on design far beyond their short life (essentially the early 1920s).

The basic unit employed by the Constructivists was a multi-functional kiosk, generally incorporating a screen, a speaker's podium, loudspeakers and accommodation for the distribution of literature and pamphlets. Gustav Klutsis' 1922 design for a screen-tribune-kiosk for the Fourth Congress of the Comintern and the fifth anniversary of the October Revolution is an absolute classic of its type. Stripped down to a skeleton of red and black struts and crowned with a screen tilted towards the ground, the stand is a fantastically sophisticated piece of agitprop which has kept its power, directness and simplicity intact. It is easy to see how these deceptively simple forms could have seduced Left-leaning Modernists throughout the world.

Another design for a propaganda stand from the same year presages the collapsing forms of deconstruction. It is crowned by the minimalist English inscription 'Workers World Unite'. The screen is to the right and marked 'screen' (ekran) in Russian Cyrillic characters. It is worth remembering that these stands are contemporary with the excesses of gilded historicism and the beginnings of architectural exoticism in Western cinema design.

These works of agitprop were shoddily constructed from any available materials – generally painted timber, cable and canvas – and their generic impermanence meant that very few survived. Yet their imagery has exerted a remarkably powerful effect on cinema architects – more noticeably on signage and advertising than on the physical fabric of the buildings themselves. As we have seen, the outrageously overscaled sign atop Duiker's Cineac could be regarded as a response to agitprop sloganeering, and, ironically, many of the huge, Las Vegas-style signs built on the Bolshevik Constructivist tradition.

During the 1930s Modernism began to take a firmer grip on the architectural avant-garde but, by and large, cinema owners and builders remained wary of the functionalist roots of Modernism. The first significant inroads by Modernist architects into commercial cinema design were made in Germany, and it is Erich Mendelsohn whose influence proved the most far-reaching, particularly in Britain. I have chosen to include a brief analysis of his designs in the section on Expressionism, although it could just as easily be slotted in at this point in the Modernist narrative. Other architects who emerged from an Expressionist background went on to lay the foundations of the functional cinema. Poelzig was key among these (he too is discussed in the Expressionist chapter) but so was Max Taut, whose prescient 1926 design for the Kino Palast remained unbuilt yet foreshadowed the developments of the 1950s and the work of Ernö Goldfinger and others. Fritz Nathan's ultra-functionalist

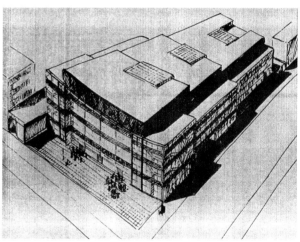

FROM TOP: Cinema Metropole, Brussels, 1930–32
Design for Kino Palast, Max Taun, 1926

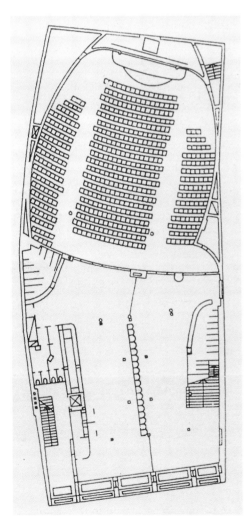

Universum in Mannheim (1929) dominated the streetscape with an imposingly pure Modernist tower. Lajos Kozma's Atrium Cinema in Budapest (1935) is another fine example of the purist functional approach, here in a mixed-use block incorporating apartments above the cinema. All the design elements, from the neons and signage to the glass doors which dominate the street frontage and the band of windows to the bar on the first floor, are expressed on the facade and seamlessly integrated into an economical and rational elevation. It remains one of the finest Modernist cinemas.

There was a period in the 1930s when Art Deco mated with Modernism, resulting in a mongrel progeny of wildly varying success. Henri Belloc's Gaumont in Paris (exact date unknown) was one of the better examples of this genre while Adrien Blomme's remarkable Cinema Metropole (1930-32) in Brussels blended functionalism and a kind of futuristic Deco aesthetic to create a building which would have looked at home in Fritz Lang's *Metropolis* or Laszlo Moholy-Nagy's oddly Constructivist sets for *Things to Come*. It has now been badly converted into a department store.

As the decade drew on, the best cinemas began to be defined by a kind of expressionistic streamlining (Moderne), which drew its power from massing and composition of architectural forms against the skyline. Neither functionalist nor Expressionist in the proper sense, these stuctures represented perhaps the last recognisable international genre of cinema architecture.

Classic Modernist architecture, however, is now beginning to make a belated appearance on the cinema scene. With the return of the city-centre cinema, urban sophisticates are prompting a return to functionalist imagery. In England in particular, David Chipperfield's Manchester Cornerhouse (1997) and much of the work of Burrell Foley Fischer and Panter Hudspith return to a kind of Modernism rarely seen in cinema architecture when functionalism was avant-garde. Modernism has finally reached cinema architecture.

Atrium, Budapest, 1935, front view and plan

EXPRESSIONISM – FILM AND ARCHITECTURE

Film was invented and developed at around the same time as psychoanalysis. The two new ways of seeing each had a critical effect on each other. Film, with its new language of flashbacks, dream scenes, animation, cutting and editing, and moving freely within time as well as space, provided people with a new way of seeing their lives and place within the world and helped them to understand the dream theories propounded by Freud, Jung and others. Psychoanalysis enabled cinema audiences to understand some of the complex editing and fantasy scenes within films. The discovery of the subconscious and the increasing importance of dreams was also instrumental in the development of new artistic modes of expression. Suddenly traditional pictorial techniques which depicted forms naturalistically yet ignored inner states of being, moods and dreams, seemed pitifully inadequate. It was largely due to this dissatisfaction with realism, as a limiting concept in the arts, that first Symbolism and then Expressionism were born in the last years of the nineteenth century and the early years of the twentieth.

Expressionism allowed artists to express the inner states of their subjects through abstracted, often dream-like art. It was originally a literary and artistic movement and its application to the solid, functional world of architecture was an odd and sometimes uncomfortable meeting. Yet the innovations of Expressionist architects in creating a new language of built form for the cinema has proved perhaps the most lasting and the most powerful of influences on subsequent generations of architects.

Expressionism was an almost entirely Germanic phenomenon. Only the Dutch developed anything like the sophistication and originality of German Expressionism and it is in Amsterdam that the first truly expressionistic cinema can be found. The Tuschinski is the absurd and endlessly amusing junction of Art Nouveau and Expressionism. Built between 1918-20 by Henri Louis de Jong, it is an incredible fantasy swarming with animals and abstract figures, its lavishly polychromatic interior dripping with eccentric detail. More highly decorated than the largely brick architecture of the Amsterdam School (many members of which were involved in its ornamentation) and completely different to what was going on anywhere else, it stands out as one of the marvels of twentieth-century cinema design. But the Tuschinski was a one-off. The serious business of Expressionism took place in Germany.

Germany after 1918 was a broken nation, devastated by war and humiliated by its outcome. The Liberal Weimar government was barely able to contain the powerful revolutionary forces that hammered it from both the Left and the Right. Artists, writers, architects and film-makers were all looking at how to create new worlds, whether idealistic cities of crystal and glass (Paul Scheerbart and Bruno Taut) or harrowingly grim depictions of inner worlds with their attendant menace and perversion. A number of producers, directors and artists had collaborated to create Expressionist worlds on the stage (including Max Reinhardt and Oskar Kokoschka), where actors, sets and lighting all struggled against naturalism to create distorted worlds of anguish and torment. As the impetus moved from theatre to cinema, the screen became the vehicle for new Expressionist experiments around 1920.

Germany's film industry actually benefited from the economic insecurity of the post-war period. The weakness of the currency and the low cost of labour and materials meant that home-produced films were far cheaper than imported American movies. The film industry was encouraged by the government and was able to remain fertile ground for avant-garde artists and directors in a way that was almost inconceivable elsewhere in the world. In a climate of severe economic depression,

Tuschinski, Amsterdam, 1918–20

architects had few chances to build the expressionistic structures of their dreams, particularly as their visions were often more suited to paper than to physical reality. Film, however, presented no such obstacles – whole visionary worlds could be created and many of the greatest and most original architects of 1920s Germany saw their impossible dreams realised on celluloid.

For Expressionist cinema, 1920 was the defining year. *The Cabinet of Dr Caligari* and *Genuine – The Tragedy of a Strange House* (both directed by Robert Wiene), and *The Golem* (directed by Paul Wegener), presented audiences with absurd worlds of stark, angular shadows, fragmented, exploding space and dark, brooding scenes closer to the primal fear of nightmares than to the harmless entertainment to which they were accustomed. The designer of the twisted, expressionistic sets portraying a dream-like version of medieval Prague in *The Golem* was Hans Poelzig. Poelzig's designs exerted a huge influence on cinema architects over the following years. In 1919 Poelzig had been employed by theatrical producer and impresario Max Reinhardt to design a new theatre from the shell of an old market hall. The result was the fantastic Grosse Schauspielhaus in Berlin. This was a theatre of fantastic stalactites, a profoundly weird auditorium which embraced the audience in an icy grip of deep shadows and Gothic forms. Reinhardt was famous for creating magical scenes on stage that involved the audience in an engrossing world of dreams and unreality. Poelzig somehow managed to create the perfect arena for this unreality – a fairy-tale grotto seating 5,000 and accommodating a vast stage thrust into the audience.

Poelzig's Expressionist masterpiece, one of the defining moments of the period, proved inspirational in its extravagant reinterpretation of the auditorium as a magical, fantastic place. Its influence can be felt powerfully in the auditorium of Ernest Wamsley Lewis's New Victoria Cinema in London (now in use as a theatre). Wamsley Lewis had studied under Poelzig in Berlin and the influence of his master was much in evidence. The odd, shell-like fountains of Poelzig's interior reappeared in London as stacks of dramatic lighting enveloping the audience in a dreamy, fantasy interior. Wamsley Lewis did not resort to the usual stagy gimmickry of the atmospheric or exotic interiors but rather created a series of architectural effects that combined elements of Modernism, Art Deco and Expressionism. The exterior of the New Victoria, however, betrays altogether different influences. Sleek, with horizontal bands introducing a kind of streamlining, while vertical fluting emphasises the main entrance, the elevations are a homage to another kind of Expressionism altogether, one which would, in the long term, become more influential than Poelzig's early version. In its seemingly paradoxical blend of functionalism with an expressionistic, sculptural architectural language, this other kind of Expressionism owed its existence to another German pioneer, Erich Mendelsohn.

Mendelsohn's Universum Cinema in Berlin (1928) is among the most influential cinemas ever built. It incorporates elements of a number of 'isms' which were vying for attention in this vibrant period in the development of architecture. Mendelsohn's zeal and passion for the building were eloquently expressed in a poem which he composed for its opening. It is an odd verse which encapsulates Expressionism perhaps better than did the cinema itself. It is worth reproducing in its entirety as one of the fullest expressions of the ambitions of the architecture of the era:

Cinema?
Pictures, theatre of motion!
Motion is life,
Real life is genuine, simple and true,
Therefore no affectation, no sentimentality.
Not in the pictures, not on the screen, not in the
    building,
Show what it contains, what it is and what its own
    limitations are.
Theatre? – Not at all!
Elevator for the screen when the sketch is succeeded
    by the film.
Advertisement tower – Artificial architecture? – on
    the contrary!
Ventilation outlets (change of air, three times an
    hour) go straight out in the direction of the
    Kurfürstendamm:
For there we are: Universum – the whole world – the
    facades of a palace? – And the profitability: shops
    make money, offices vivify the scene and procure a
    public.
Porch entrance for high society?
Mouth opened wide and flooded with light,
    decorated in splendour.
For – you are to go in, everyone – into life, to the
    film, to the pay-box!
Cathedral cupolas? What for! Tortoise-shaped roof,
    projecting curves of the sloping ceiling, going
    towards the screen wall.
Ah! Camera!

New Victoria (now Apollo Victoria), 1930, auditorium and exterior

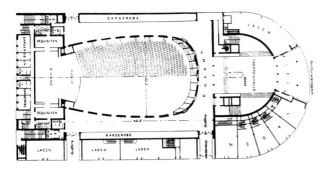

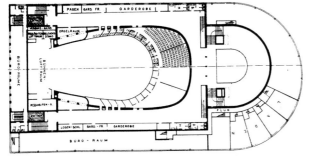

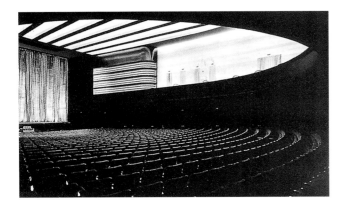

FROM TOP: Design for a film studio, Erich Mendelsohn, 1918
Universum, Berlin, Erich Mendelsohn, 1928

Right!

Screen – the outside world.

Pictures – the bright life, circus and moonlight at the seaside.

We spectators – one thousand, two thousand retinas, which suck up and reflect, each one happy or living an experience. Thus, no Rococo castle for Buster Keaton, no stucco pastries for *Potemkin* and *Scapa Flow*.

But, also, no fear!

No sober reality, no claustrophobia of life-weary brain acrobats –

Fantasy!

Fantasy – but no lunatic asylum – dominated by space, colour and light.

Under the swinging circle of the foyer, the street disappears, under the conical beams of the ceiling lights, the haze of evening disappears.

Then – left or right pass by the beacon of the pay-box into the twilight of the passage – Here you surely meet 'them'.

Bend down in tension!

Compressor!

But then full speed.

All planes, curves and light-waves flash from the ceiling to the screen through the medium of music into the flickering image – into the Universe.

Mendelsohn's brand of Expressionism had evolved from its organic, curvaceous mode into a more severe, functionalist approach which nevertheless retained the dynamic, sculptural qualities of his early buildings, such as the Einstein Tower at Potsdam (1920-24). The elemental, striking appearance of the Universum seems to come straight out of one of Mendelsohn's evocative sketches or his simplified, stripped-down poetry. His sketch for a film studio from 1918 shows an almost fully developed version of his expressionistic streamlining. The curving, dynamic lines reappear, albeit in simplified form, at the Universum. Very unusually for a cinema building, the external form of the Universum referred to the shape of what was going on inside, a point he makes in his poetry, sneering at contemporary 'Rococo castles'. The horseshoe-shaped auditorium was expressed in a sleek, wrap-around curve and the continuous ribbon window that followed it all around, illuminating the circulation spaces that encircled the auditorium. A slim fin broke through this curve, affording space for advertising and lighting. This architectonic device would prove hugely influential in later cinema buildings and, converted into a central tower, became almost a bedrock of the streamlined style.

In his auditorium, too, Mendelsohn pioneered the streamlining which would come to dominate theatre design in the next decade. The whole interior seemed to be rushing at speed towards the screen; slick, illuminated lines gave directionality to the interior and a sense of artifice and excitement while never detracting from the focus of the space, the screen.

Mendelsohn's version of expressive streamlining greatly influenced buildings during the 1930s. His buildings, perhaps curiously, struck a deep chord with British cinema architects, although the country as a whole was entirely immune to the sculptural excesses of Expressionism. Mendelsohn's curving, sketch-like forms were a clear reference for W E Trent's Gaumont Palace, Wolverhampton (1932), which showed elements of Expressionist detailing in its stripped elevations and elegant auditorium and in the Frankenstein's laboratory lights which surmount the entrance. Alistair Gladstone Macdonald's sleek and dynamic newsreel theatre built within Victoria Station (1934) was a fine example of how this curvaceous aesthetic could be used to create a recognisable image for the cinema. The architect of the Bristol News Theatre of 1933 borrowed heavily from the forms of Wamsley Lewis's New Victoria to create a slick, black, modernistic facade reminiscent of contemporary radio designs – perhaps in order to qualify this as a news venue rather than pure entertainment.

Another architect profoundly influenced by Mendelsohn's sketch-like visions was Rudolf Frankel. The Lichtburg in Berlin (1929-30) was one of the finest twentieth-century cinemas, a powerful composition of sensuously curving and rigidly straight elements with an exquisitely carved-out auditorium, full of motion yet dramatically simple. It is a building that perfectly demonstrates the difficulties in trying to separate out the strands of Expressionism, Modernism and Moderne in the development of cinema design. His less well-known Scala Cinema in Bucharest (1938) wraps curvaceously around the urban block in a single sweep, its facade a paper-thin plane. The interiors reflect the curve of the elevation in every wall surface and counter. Its cornerless spaces seem to echo the seamlessness of the screen and the curving balcony and seating in the deep, fan-shaped auditorium. Other cinemas heavily influenced by Mendelsohn's sleek curving lines include Gutierrez Soto's Europa and Barcelo cinemas in Madrid (1927-29 and 1930 respectively). In fact the economy and elegance of

TOP and MIDDLE: Gaumont Palace, Wolverhampton, 1932
BOTTOM: Newsreel Theatre, Victoria Station, 1934

TOP ROW: Bristol News Theatre, 1933 (left) and Capitol Cinema, Berlin, 1926 (auditorium)
MIDDLE AND BOTTON ROW: Scala Cinema, Bucharest, 1937 exterior, auditorium, plan and lobby

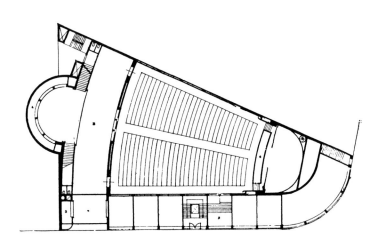

streamlining ensured Mendelsohn's influence over a number of interesting Spanish and Italian designs from the late 1920s to the early 1940s. The Universum itself was badly damaged during the Second World War and it is an irony that one of the defining monuments in the breakaway from the traditional theatrical architectural idiom should have found itself rebuilt and restructured for use as a live theatre.

While Mendelsohn was redefining Expressionism by blending its dynamism with the rigour of functionalism in his sleek Universum, the senior Expressionist, Poelzig, had moved away from his visionary roots. In 1926, the year Mendelsohn started designing the Universum, Poelzig was completing the Capitol in Berlin. Serious and rational, this was almost a return to the monumental architecture of his German forebears, Friedrich Gilly and Karl Friedrich Schinkel. The elevation was a simple composition of two storeys subdivided by a series of mullions. The structure was capped by an octagonal drum, which appears as the residual dome from traditional German opera houses. Simple and severe, the Capitol was typically Teutonic. A practical and functional response to its urban site, it was a very fine building which demonstrated that a cinema could make itself obvious in an urban setting (while blending in), without resorting to kitsch decoration. In its symmetrical severity, the Capitol was closely related to Fritz Wilms' Piccadilly Theatre, built a year earlier in 1925. This monumental building presented a regal facade to the street with a huge glazed opening at its centre. It was lifted above the surrounding buildings by a spiky series of battlements which were characteristic of a number of German and Austrian Expressionist buildings, although appeared here in a more restrained Classicised form.

By the end of the 1920s the first explosion of Expressionism had faded. Its best exponents, such as Poelzig and Mendelsohn, had become proponents of functionalism and Modernist orthodoxy. Yet expressionistic motifs remained a staple of cinema architects. While elsewhere the architecture of the 1930s brought either a stark Modernist aesthetic, Art Deco frivolity or, increasingly as the decade grew older, bombastic Classicism, cinema design remained one of the few areas where architects were able to use a powerfully expressionistic and sculptural language.

Julian Leathart's Dreamland in Margate (1935), a cinema and proto-theme-park complex, blended the brick Expressionism of Dutch architecture with ideas culled from Mendelsohn and Berlin to create a new kind of Odeon style. The constant conflict of

Dreamland, Margate

horizontals and verticals created a dynamic and sculptural mass which ensured the building dominated its setting. Andrew Mather's Odeon, Chingford (also 1935), was a fantastic composition which used expressionistic streamlining to create a massive and impressive composition of shooting verticals in gleaming white stone. Harry Weedon would follow with a series of cinemas that were undoubtedly expressionistic but not quite Expressionist. These works fit more neatly into the next section which will briefly examine the emerging language of the Moderne, a peculiar style of toned-down Modernism which gained its dynamism and populism from its striking appropriation of the language of Expressionism.

The last few years have seen a revival of architecture with expressionistic overtones. Coop Himmelb(l)au's Dresden UFA cinema blends the language of deconstruction with the jagged, crystalline fantasies of German Expressionism, while Tom Kovac and Geoff Malone's futuristic but intriguing design for the French Generic Cinema can be easily slotted into the biomorphic and organic traditions of Expressionist architecture. With the domination of the blind box and the cartoon-infested lobby, the world of cinema architecture seems ripe for an Expressionist revival. In fact, the cinema's very genesis in the fairgrounds and in seedy, crowded halls, its status as an escapist realm of fantasy, and its reliance on light and sound to the exclusion of the outside world, would seem to conspire to create the ideal breeding ground for the emergence of a new Expressionism. About time too.

THE MODERNE CINEMA – STREAMLINING AND LIGHT ARCHITECTURE

The classic Art Deco cinema of the 1930s was essentially still a theatre decorated with a new blend of Parisian and Hollywood motifs. The experiments of Expressionist architects in Germany demonstrated that the cinema could be a generator of new architectural forms. The abandonment of the traditional theatrical model in favour of streamlined, sculptural structures inspired architects elsewhere to re-examine the architectural manifestation of the cinema.

Two buildings in particular were responsible for a new approach to architectural massing which was to define cinema architecture during the 1930s. Both were completed in 1928 and both are in Berlin: the first, Erich Mendelsohn's Universum is briefly discussed in the essay on Expressionism; the second, Schöffler, Scholoenbach and Jacobi's Titania Palast was massed in an even more sculptural and dramatic fashion than the Universum. The Titania Palast was also the first building conceived in terms of *Lichtarchitektur* (Light Architecture). By day the cinema is a blocky, rather heavy, masonry structure which defines a busy street corner. At night, however, the building becomes a shining beacon, the architecture dissolving into a brilliantly lit nocturnal sculpture, centring on a slim tower. Alternating bright and dark stripes on the tower create an effect similar to Mendelsohn's evocative thumbnail sketches, with bands wrapping themselves around a dynamic tower, emphasising its height against the blocky mass of the walls. A concealed light beneath the eaves illuminates the Titania Palast's name so that the building itself is the signage; architecture, light and symbol are integrated with no need for extra billboards to spoil the profile of the carefully considered structure. The auditorium, in marked contrast to the blockiness of the elevations, features an incredibly dynamic series of swooping curves, creating an almost tunnel-like effect and the hint of a proscenium, or perhaps a sequence of concentric lenses. This proved an electrifyingly influential building – it is not an overstatement to say that its impact is still being felt in cinema architecture. In Britain in particular the Titania Palast was the catalyst for an unprecedented wave of cinema building in the 1930s as well as being the influence behind what has become known as the Odeon style.

The undisputed master of the Odeons was Harry Weedon, who developed a uniquely recognisable language of modernistic cinema architecture. Abandoning the decorative excesses of the exotic theatres and the historicist fantasies which had dominated large-scale cinema architecture in Britain until the early 1930s (and which remained in the cinema architects' palette of styles, as with Komisarjevsky), Weedon built cinemas on an industrial scale. The buildings seemed to be streamlined in order to process as many people as possible through their huge foyers and into the auditoria. A series of fantastic, landmark buildings by Weedon and others positioned the cinema in an often featureless suburban landscape in which the bright neon signs and expressionistic fins and towers enjoyed a virtual monopoly on the skyline. Odeons in Chingford, North London, and Kingstanding, Birmingham (both 1935), and in Colwyn Bay in the north of Wales, Sutton Coldfield near Birmingham, Muswell Hill and Well Hall (north and south London respectively), Lancaster and Scarborough (all 1936) are among the finest British buildings of the century.

The Modernist establishment's disdain of this kind of populist Moderne architecture is epitomised by Nikolaus Pevsner's comment at the end of the chapter on theatres in *A History of Building Types*: 'In Britain in

the 1930s a jazzy Modernism dominated. The most successful architect in that objectionable vein was Harry Weedon.' Certainly these buildings were far from perfect. They were churned out at such a rate that the ink on the drawings barely had time to dry before the cinemas were complete. The typically functionalist criticism that these buildings were more wilful sculptural indulgences than serious, rational responses can also be justifiably levelled. But these criticisms seem to miss the point that a critical part of the function of the cinema is to advertise itself. These were buildings which announced themselves as up to date and fashionable, places for a good time in an often drab semi-urban landscape. Streamlining may have derived from an enthusiasm for speed and been applied at first to aircraft and cars, but it later came to be used on anything from fridges to cigarette lighters, so why not cinemas?

Although this kind of sculptural Moderne remained dominant in the suburbs throughout the late 1930s in Britain, another more urban variation stuck closer to the Light Architecture which had been developed by the Germans. Harry Weedon and Andrew Mather together designed the Odeon Leicester Square (1937), which remains London's most familiar cinema. Its blocky massing and bold geometric forms ensure that it stands out during the day, the black stone facing marking it out as the Square's most prominent inhabitant. At night however, the black disappears against the darkness of the sky, and the strips of light and signage and the brightness of the double-height entrance shine out across the Square, reversing the building's polarity. The stark solidity of the dark stone gives way to a streamlined interior composed of interlocking layers, like the shell of an armadillo, focusing on a pair of abstracted breaking waves carved into the walls which ripple through the interior

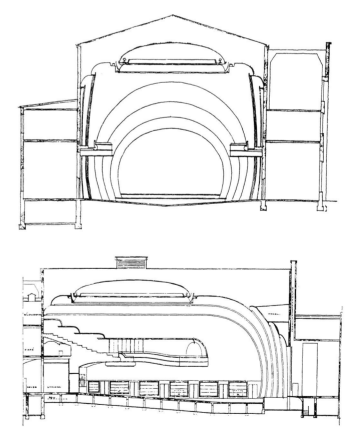

Titania Palast, Berlin, 1928
Exterior, auditorium, sections

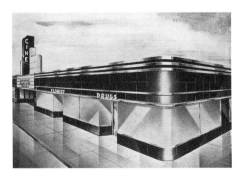

Magazine adverts from the 1930s featuring cinemas including Odeon, Chingford (second from top)

behind rows of curious nude dancers who appear to break through the sound barrier in their haste to reach the screen.

While Britain had the prodigious Harry Weedon, the States had S Charles Lee, an architect who played an equally pivotal role in defining a whole country's cinema architecture. Lee had cut his teeth on fanciful, exotic and Classically styled theatres on the West Coast in the early 1930s. He went through a phase of designing some of the definitive masterpieces of Art Deco cinema design and onto a type of small, suburban cinema which was the equivalent of Weedon's Odeons in Britain. These tended to be small, streamlined structures centred around a central shaft. This tower feature would exhibit some form of neon signage, usually with vertical lettering which would create a striking feature in the flat, attenuated suburbs of California. The State Theatre in San Diego (1941) is a fine example of Lee's *oeuvre*, with a lit-up tower reminiscent of the overblown laboratory sets in *The Bride of Frankenstein* (1935), while the corkscrew tower of his absurd Academy Theatre, also in San Diego (1939), is among the most memorably oddball and eye-catching devices ever to be tacked onto a cinema building. Whereas the British movie theatres of the late 1930s strove for a kind of urban monumentality and massive solidity, Lee's cinemas, and those of his contemporaries, were proudly suburban; small in scale, with their vertical shafts designed to be seen from the road. This is the kind of billboard architecture that we now tend to associate with Las Vegas and from which Robert Venturi told us we ought to learn.

Although his work defined the genre, Lee was by no means the only architect designing in this style. In fact, by the mid-to-late 1930s it had become the ubiquitous American suburban style. Virtually every Main Street in Smalltown, USA retains a sculptural tower or streamlined frontage; Oak Park, Illinois' Lake Theater, designed by Thomas Lamb in 1936, is illustrated here as a fine example of this curvy, expressionistic style. Even the king of the atmospherics, John Eberson, was designing streamlined cinemas by 1938; the Bethesda Theater (just outside Washington DC) is typical of his suburban output, while the Colony Theater in Cleveland is a superb example of the apex of streamlined design.

The English version of streamline Moderne remained more Classical in its influences. Less curvaceous, less influenced by automobile design, a

CLOCKWISE FROM TOP LEFT: Egyptian Theatre, Sioux Falls, 1938; Train-carriage-shaped auditorium, Victoria Newsreel Theatre; Waterloo Station Newsreel Cinema, early 1930s; State Theater, San Diego, 1941; Lake Theatre, Oak Park; Warner Cinema, Leicester Square, London, current state; Warner Cinema, Leicester Square, London, 1938

typical example is Edward Stone's facade to the Warner Cinema in Leicester Square (1938), which manages to blend Deco, *Lichtarchitektur* and Moderne gestures in a single, relatively narrow elevation. Streamlining in Britain was more usually applied to other new building types, particularly garages and buildings to do with locomotion, bus stations and the like. The exception was in the news cinemas which cropped up often near, or in, railway stations in the 1930s. The closeness to travel gave some justification to the speed-derived curving lines of the streamline style. News cinemas at Waterloo and Victoria stations, both now pointlessly destroyed, were the best examples.

This spectacular wave of glamorous cinema building was brought to an abrupt end by the outbreak of war in 1939. The bulky, monumental masses of Britain's suburban Odeons must have looked overweight and obsolete by the end of the war. Once the opportunity arose for cinema building to recommence, Modernism had become the orthodoxy. New cinemas were built beneath huge office complexes or buried in shopping centres. The slim, neon-lit towers of the suburban American movie theatre, however, seemed the embodiment of the American automotive lifestyle. It proved easy for this style of Moderne American cinema to metamorphose in the immediate post-war years (which were, of course, prosperous in contrast to the grim rationing of leisure in Europe) into the louche 1950s roadside theatre and ultimately into the drive-in, where the architecture was often confined to the billboard alone.

LEFT, FROM TOP: Odeon, Morecambe, 1937
Odeon, Colwyn Bay, 1936
Odeon Leicester Square, London, current state
Odeon Leicester Square, London, 1937
BELOW: Design for a streamlined auditorium, 1930s, USA

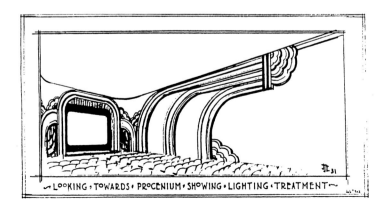

THE LATE TWENTIETH-CENTURY CINEMA

The decades that followed the Second World War saw a sharp erosion of the cinema as an architectural type. The cinema did not disappear, but it often became subsumed into other, larger buildings or became an ever-simpler set of basic units which could be easily reproduced in any setting. Television and subsequently video and other forms of home entertainment were, and still are, consistently used as excuses to minimise expenditure on cinema architecture so that distributors could create viable businesses. This seems absurd when it is precisely the experience of watching a film in a stimulating social environment that differentiates cinema from the small screen. The decline in audiences also left cities with a surplus of cinemas, including enormous super-cinemas which were often subdivided, spoiling the architectural effect of these grand theatres. Thousands of buildings which had been at the hub of the community only a couple of decades earlier were demolished. There was no demand for new cinemas except in out-of-town and suburban locations where the arrival of malls created a new need for all entertainments under a single roof.

The drive-in was the perfect manifestation of the non-architecture of mid-twentieth century cinema design. The only real architecture was the billboard, and this was often expressive and sculptural, becoming the natural extension of the streamlined, late Deco cinemas of the early 1940s. Among the more interesting of these were the buildings of S Charles Lee, whose designs now seem remarkably prescient, some anticipating the tilted structures, huge glazed walls and Las Vegas-style signs which have again become popular (see Jon Jerde's Star City in Birmingham). With its pair of concrete arches, tilted signage and large canopy, the Baldwin Theater (1949) in LA, California, designed by Lewis Wilson, perfectly demonstrates the erosion of the structure in favour of the sign. The building itself becomes invisible.

Once the new cinema ceased to be an element in the urban landscape and its object became the attraction of drivers along a freeway, cinema architecture declined almost entirely into billboard design. This is not to dismiss entirely the architecture of the drive-in, which has its own rather minimal charm as well as the powerful stimulant of nostalgia for a generation that would later wield great influence.

There have been surprisingly few innovations in cinema architecture since its inception over a century ago, and even those early cinemas were based on previous forms, including the theatre and the sideshow. The innovations that have been successful tend to have been those to do with economies of scale. The contribution of the late twentieth century to cinema architecture has been the multiplex and the megaplex – sprawling sheds full of boxy auditoria and popcorn stands.

The multiplexes and megaplexes that emerged in the 1970s and which dominated the new cinema building boom of the 1980s reduced the architectural element to the design of a garish, stick-on facade and lobby. The purpose of these lurid lobbies was to sell as much food as possible to cinema-goers, rather than to impress with any sense of grandeur or atmosphere. Their location in the deepest 'burbs allowed developers to get away with a far less sophisticated level of design than if they had been built in cities. The multiplexes have tended to be the most basic sheds, built by developers (with minimal involvement by architects) and then fitted out by the film chains. In this way the architecture is limited to interior design and, at best, some kind of canopy. This pattern remains among the most popular forms of cinema building.

Odeon, Elephant and Castle, London, 1965

ABC Putney, 1975, the joyless face of late modernism

Another innovation, which similarly succeeds in squeezing out the very notion of cinema architecture, has been the placing of a cinema within a larger, usually commercial structure. In the 1950s and 60s the pattern was set by the builders of the ubiquitous urban glass and steel office blocks which included a cinema buried somewhere deep in their bowels. This was in part due to advances in the technology of projection and the improved quality of film stock, which became much more fireproof, allowing the integration of cinema buildings into bigger complexes in a way that would have been a fire hazard only a few years earlier. The reason was also partly (in fact, mostly) economical. Offices generated more rental income on prestigious downtown sites than cinemas did and modern buildings with deep floor-plates contained deep, lightless spaces at their centres that proved useless for habitation or office functions but ideal for cinemas. The Curzon Cinema in Mayfair, London, designed by Sir John Burnet, Tait and Partners in 1966, is a fine modern design which replaced a better one from the 1930s by the same architects. This is a rare example of a good structure of this type, its interior enlivened by an unusual coffered ceiling in the auditorium designed by Op Artist Viktor Vasarely. The ABC Cinema in Putney, by Richard Siefert (1975) is a perfect example of the bottom end of this kind of development. Now these kinds of developments tend to be located within malls rather than offices so that even the restrained (if dull) elegance of the Curzon is lost.

There were, however, some worthy efforts at redefining cinema architecture in the immediate post-war years. Ernö Goldfinger's Odeon at the Elephant and Castle in London (1965) was an expressive and sculptural effort, though far from beautiful (now scandalously demolished). A number of German cinema architects working in the 1950s seemed on the verge of reinventing the auditorium with expressionistic curvy balconies and dramatic lighting effects but these seemed to lead nowhere in the longer term. The same can be said for those branches of cinema architecture in which architects were given a freer hand – the international exhibition cinemas. In many ways, some of the most interesting developments in building for films have derived from the quest for novelty that characterises the international merry-go-round of the expos, but these buildings fall largely outside the scope of this book, which is dedicated to the movie theatre as a distinct type, a place for entertainment. However, as with Le Corbusier's much-lauded Philips Pavilion at the Brussels World Fair of 1958, so with the IMAX cinemas currently being erected in remarkable numbers in scientific institutions and museums throughout the world, the impetus for radical cinema design has come from the market for a blend of education and entertainment. These buildings, however, seem to me to be part of a different subject, as much museum as cinema, and it seems reasonable to treat them separately.

LEFT AND ABOVE: Curzon Cinema, London, 1966
BELOW: Balwin Theatre, LA, 1949

INSTITUTIONAL CINEMA – MUSEUMS, IMAX AND PLANETARIA

From recording the exact motion of the legs of racing horses to documenting journeys to outer and inner space, film has, throughout its history, been presented as the perfect medium for conveying scientific knowledge to the masses without boring them. Only recently has the role of film become almost pure entertainment, with the advent of television and affordable international travel, and, the disappearance of the cinema's role as newsgiver and conveyor of images from inaccessible places and trouble spots. The roots of the cinema lie precisely in its ability to record events which people could otherwise only read about – if they could read at all. Film became a medium for entertainment only when its potential as more than a mere record was realised and the idea of narrative in film became understood. On the other hand, film has always been mistrusted as an educational medium; perhaps it is too accessible, too much fun, too easy. It is also infinitely malleable.

From the earliest days of newsreels in the silent cinema, historic events were specially staged and relayed as the real thing. It proved the ideal vehicle for propaganda, as television is today. Many critics feel that modern war, for the West at least, is primarily a media event, staged for and consumed by TV. This cynicism can be traced way back to the early years of the century when battles and war scenes were recreated to show the right kind of heroism and not the bloody, mindless brutality of war. The mistrust of film engendered by early frauds lives on in conspiracy theories: it is still maintained, often quite credibly, that NASA never went to the moon in 1969 but rather staged the whole event on a film set. The early emergence, for instance, of special effects, the ease of editing and staging for film, and the enthusiasm of audiences for the astonishing have conspired to tarnish film's credibility.

Yet despite these reservations, film remains an important, often indispensable tool in education, and it has, of course, become an academic field in its own right. Repertory cinemas and art-houses revel in their mind-broadening role, a status far above mere entertainment. The development of film as an educational medium has led to an array of buildings that contain auditoria or cinemas but which are not cinemas in the accepted sense. These fall slightly outside the scope of this book, yet it would be impossible to dismiss these buildings altogether, so I have included a few interesting examples as an appendix to the traditional notion of the movie palace.

Museums, universities and international exhibitions have housed much of the most dramatic cinema architecture of recent years. In some ways such cinemas are really extensions of the buildings and building types to which they are attached, but in others they are worth looking at as a valuable influence which could be fed back to the broader sphere of the public cinema as a place of entertainment.

This kind of interchange has been occurring since the pre-cinema era. The cinema's predecessors were the dioramas, panoramas and camera obscuras of the nineteenth century. The forms of these buildings derived from their functions: a diorama required a cylinder or rotunda, while other forms of what has unfortunately come to be known as 'edutainment' may have required domes or even spheres. Later shows, from animations to magic lanterns, were dressed up in historical costume, Egyptian, Roman and so on, to emphasise the depth of the mysteries within and the eternal truths that would be revealed. These buildings needed to attract people and their architecture was used to do just that. As moving film arrived it was presented in the successors of these buildings and at fairgrounds as something to astound

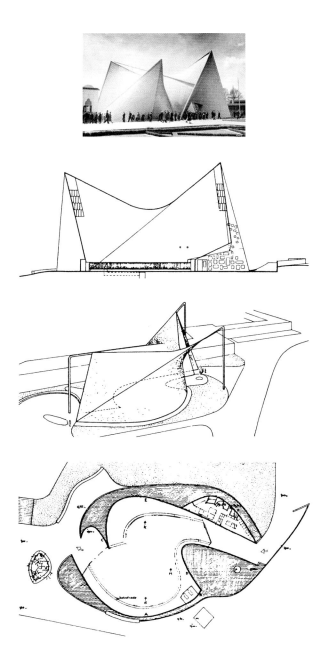

Philips Pavilion, Brussels World Fair, 1958

and entertain. But film had to compete with other entertainments, from theatre to alcohol and, whether in grand halls or extravagantly decorated booths, it had to attract an audience with the promise of enlightenment.

From the Great Globe built in 1851 in London's Leicester Square (a building competing with the nearby Great Exhibition in Hyde Park, the proto-world expo) to Le Corbusier's Philips Pavilion (*La poème électronique*) at the Brussels World Fair of 1958, to Denis Laming's Boeing IMAX in Seattle (1998) and 3-D IMAX at the Futuroscope Park in Poitiers, France, there is a history of visionary architectural forms being used to express new cinematic technologies and media. The IMAX is perhaps the most interesting recent example of this trend. Sitting slightly uneasily between entertainment and education, this format has hitherto often been limited to museums and institutions – the cumbersome filming equipment and huge size of the film reels means that it has so far been inappropriate for dramatic productions and remains best suited to documentaries and documentary records (such as trips to space or underwater exploration). Yet it has been the catalyst for a number of truly remarkable buildings in recent years. In an environment where the major players in the cinema industry are still over-keen on building huge out-of-town megaplexes, squeezing cinemas into crushingly monotonous serviced sheds, architects jump at the chance to design these interesting new cinemas in which they can express something of the auditorium in the architecture. It is a rare chance to re-examine the theatre as a building type and try new ideas in design and form.

Denis Laming's IMAX buildings are obvious examples of the impact of the IMAX on cinema architecture, although his ambitious and undeniably impressive forms

Education Space Science Center, Edmonton

Grande Prairie Theatre, Alberta

IMAX Theatres, Denis Laming

are often derivative of the kind of sci-fi expo architecture which peaked with Wallace K Harrison's iconic designs for the Trylon and Perisphere at the 1939 New York World's Fair. Douglas J Cardinal's sensuously curvaceous designs for the Grande Prairie Theatre in a regional college in Alberta, Canada, are an unusual example of organicism in a genre dominated by angularity. The undulating walls and balconies echo the work of Felix Candela but also presage the free-flowing sculptural forms for which Frank O Gehry has since become world famous. Cardinal's building for the Education Space Sciences Center in Edmonton, Alberta is a wonderfully absurd UFO of a building which foreshadows Page + Steele's Colossus in Toronto. Its Space Age chic is perfectly suited to its function and the building seems to

evolve naturally the bizarre-looking, alien-robot aesthetic of the projector at its core. Santiago Calatrava's designs for the sleek Science Centre at Valencia in Spain (from 1991) are another fine example of the spacey aesthetic which architects seem to find attractive for the institutional cinema. Calatrava's organic approach, like Cardinal's, seems wholly suitable for this free-standing building which is undeniably one of the most elegant shells of recent years.

The work of Fletcher Priest at London's Science Museum and at the Planetarium shows how this kind of institutional work could potentially cross over to inform the world of entertainment. If architects can make learning interesting and dramatic, they should have no trouble creating cinemas.

THE FUTURE

Nothing dates as fast as the future. Predictions are notoriously difficult. Yet a few trends are emerging which may begin to indicate a set of possible futures for cinema architecture. The most interesting of these is the return of the city-centre cinema. Saucier + Perotte's Montreal cinema and the work of Burrell Foley Fischer and Panter Hudspith in the UK all point to a renaissance of the urban cinema and to the emergence of a new, more sophisticated market. These are buildings with few flashing lights and hot dogs. A new audience has been discovered in adults rather than the adolescents and lowest common denominators who have been the ubiquitous targets of marketing people for the last few decades. Bars and bookshops look as likely to be found in urban cinemas as arcade games and burgers are in the out-of-towners. When John Travolta's Vince in *Pulp Fiction* talks of cinemas in Europe where you can get a beer, he is amazed that bars can be found in what, to Americans, is the wholesome (i.e. childish) world of the picture theatre. Yet Tarantino's character may have hit on an emerging trend. Adults want to be treated like grown-ups for the off-screen action if not the action on the screen, and the urban cinema will certainly incorporate bars as part of an overall environment and as a tool to introduce people to the cinema.

The artificial world inside the cinema may even be themed in an attempt to recreate an urban street or a European square. With the increasing mallification of Western culture one apparent future is the irony of city-centre cinemas which turn their backs on the city only to recreate an idealised, Disneyfied version of the urban street with bars, cafés and shops in a wholly artificially serviced interior. The happier version of this scenario entails cinemas becoming a part of the streetscape and their bars and foyers feeding back into urban life. Panter Hudspith's Curzon Soho and Burrell Foley Fischer's Lux (both at the epicentres of London's most self-consciously arty quarters) are fine examples of this reorientation of the cinema as hip hang-out, enticing customers with an attractive urban lounge.

The urban, adult audience demands a different setting, and the reintroduction of natural materials and Modernist motifs (even if this remains a kind of chic, corporate restaurant Modernism rather than a radical, reinterpretative Modernism) is already creating a new kind of cinema which disposes with cartoon imagery and brightly lit franchises. The concept is closer to art-house than to Art Deco, to carrot cake and coffee than to popcorn and hot dogs. This may lead to the widespread evolution of arts centres incorporating cinemas alongside theatres and galleries, which in turn could radically affect cinema style. Tim Foster's cool Tricycle is a good example of this mix. However, because such centres often feature a cinema buried deep within the complex where it is not specifically expressed in architectural terms, I have not included many.

The new urbane audience who like to get their culture in a single dose demands new levels of comfort and luxury to go with their designer beers and sushi, or whatever replaces hot dogs and popcorn. The affluent luxury cinema, which takes its cue from first and club classes in air travel – lounges with wide seats, lots of legroom, free snacks, good service and outrageous prices – is another emerging trend which may grow. Luxury is another gimmick to induce people to pay more – so important in an industry where novelty is still attractive.

As a trend that is already identifiable, there seems little danger in forecasting the continuing revival of the city-centre theatre: the future of the out-of-town multiplex is less certain. The hitherto astounding success of the megaplexes, buildings of twenty screens or more, has almost certainly peaked. Canada and the USA remain addicted to the megaplex but Europe, with a few exceptions, can probably get by without them. Where they do occur – the 1988 Kinepolis in Brussels (twenty-four screens) and the Star City in Birmingham (thirty screens) – they will probably survive, even thrive, as novelties, but they seem unlikely to spark a new tradition. A few very large cinemas are opening in big cities in Northern England. It will be interesting to see their progress. Few cities or areas can support so many screens and a return to complexes of fifteen to twenty screens at most, aimed at adolescents and families with perhaps a few screens devoted to special-interest films, seems a safe bet. With these cinemas located on city peripheries, smaller urban cinemas will cater for more mature audiences. Eastern Europe provides an interesting variation on the spread of the multiplex with the proliferation and huge success of the downtown multiplex, a pattern that is being followed in the UK with projects like the huge Printworks and Trafford Centre in Manchester. Cheaper land prices, low labour costs and huge potential audiences mean higher returns and the financial possibility of locating large cinemas in urban locations. The quality of the architecture of this potentially interesting new urban building type has yet to prove itself.

Japan experienced a huge surge in the growth of multiplexes during the 1990s and the Far East as a whole has quickly followed suit, although most of these buildings are architecturally forgettable. India, with its enormous and thriving film industry and enthusiastic audiences, has spawned very few cinemas of note. Margins are tiny but the scale of the market would seem to indicate that sooner or later something has to happen.

Major changes in technology will undoubtedly trigger a small revolution in the specialist design of cinemas, yet it is hard to forecast the effects on architecture. Digital technology will arrive with great fanfare and make projection booths redundant. This will lead to the freeing-up of space within existing cinema buildings and the removal of one of the great restrictions and perennial logistical problems for cinema architects. In existing cinemas projection booths could be converted to private balconies for hire by small parties, or perhaps booths with love seats, or, even better, hotel-style beds and room service for lazy/greedy/randy film-goers. Another possibility is the conversion of these spaces to kitchens, cafés or bars, as cinemas become social gathering places. New buildings will be cheaper and easier to construct and the lack of extensive projection facilities will bring about a unity of

space within the auditorium which could pave the way for a more coherent form of interior architecture. Sound, with the introduction of George Lucas's THX standards, will undoubtedly continue to improve and audiences will demand good sound quality, without which the outrageously complex and expensive explosions and special effects that are the *raison d'être* of so many films, can't be appreciated.

The IMAX format has been promising to become mainstream for a long time. City-centre IMAX cinemas are proliferating and the 3-D IMAX format, which demands a dome, has already led to a number of interesting buildings. For the moment, much of the best IMAX architecture is confined to institutions and tends to inhabit larger existing buildings. These can potentially inspire ingenious solutions which can feed back into the world of the free-standing cinema building.

The 1990s produced a quiet revolution in cinema architecture. For the first time in over half a century, architecturally fascinating cinemas were erected all over the world within the space of a few years. Nostalgics invariably look back to the 1930s as some kind of golden age in cinema architecture. The prominence of the 1930s as the Roman Empire of the cinema is not being challenged; its ruins and monuments still surround us and remind us of the potency of the cinema architect. The great cinema architects of the 1930s created powerful brands for the studios and distributors. Odeon style, for instance, is an instantly recognisable trademark almost solely achieved through the powerful architecture created by Harry Weedon, which defined the public perception of the cinema for at least a couple of generations. Contemporary reliance on blown-up stills, cartoon characters, garish logos and popular franchises, although colourful, is primitive in the extreme when compared with the monumental branding of the Odeons. It has not led to any buildings to match the exuberance and inventiveness of the 1930s.

But in the 1990s the reintegration of the cinema into the urban fabric has led to magnificent schemes, some from internationally renowned architects and some from architects who deserve to be better known. Coop Himmelb(l)au's Dresden cinema, Koen van Velsen's Rotterdam cinema (which may age less gracefully than the photos suggest) and Saucier + Perotte's thoughtful Montreal cinema centre, are all wonderful urban buildings which have entirely revitalised the cinema, revivifying the notion that architecture can create an identity and a brand for the cinema which acts as the finest possible billboard. They should make a difference.

If Coop Himmelb(l)au's remarkable building suggests one version of Germany's Expressionist heritage, Tom Kovac and Geoff Malone's plans for the French Generic Cinema suggest the alternative route. The spiky, crystalline fragmentation of the Dresden cinema echoes the jagged shadows and the urban angst of Expressionist film-making techniques; the Kovac/Malone design recalls the branch of early twentieth-century Expressionism that led to biomorphism, its roots stretching back to the organic fantasies of Hermann Finsterlin via Metabolism. Kovac and Malone's design is one of the few to address changing notions of the medium at every level. Its continuous surfaces and flowing spaces negate powerfully ingrained distinctions between floors, walls and ceilings, while all the surfaces become potential receptors for film and image. Its potent organicism also hints at the coming changes in perception of viewing space brought about by the much-talked-about arrival of virtual reality and interactive movies. The last vestiges of traditional theatre forms could well disappear as the relationship between the body and the space changes from passive audience to active participant. The irony is that this final, ultimate technological leap, which would create the first true revolution in cinema since the introduction of sound, may have a solely negative effect on architecture – if it demands architecture at all. The true architecture of virtual reality is the interactive bodysuit or the darkened room of sensory deprivation. The lobby, auditorium and public spaces become obsolete. After a few years this will inevitably lead to nostalgia and, perhaps, people will return to the few downtown cinemas of the 1930s still left standing.

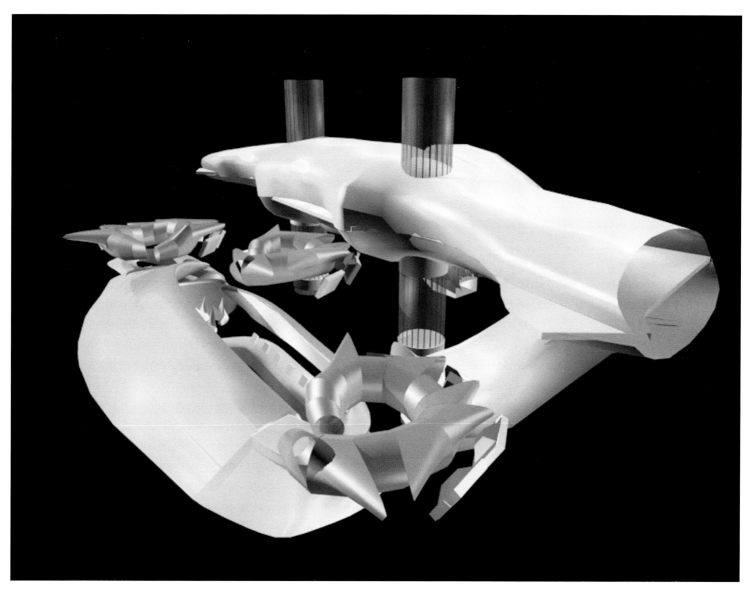

French Generic Cinema Designs, Tom Kovac and Geoff Malone

THE CINEMA IN FILM

The film industry embodies a curiously paradoxical combination of an almost infinite capacity for nostalgic self-mythologisation with a reckless disregard for its own past. The movie theatre frequently appears in films as a cipher for a lost past, a sentimental symbol of a better age. In Giuseppe Tornatore's achingly sentimental *Cinema Paradiso* (1989) the theatre itself is as much a central character as the sympathetic projectionist or the little boy fascinated by the movies. The cinema becomes home to Toto, the central character, while Philippe Noiret's projectionist becomes a surrogate father replacing the real one who never returned from the war. It is his obsession with the cinema which leads Toto to his destiny as a director and away from small-town Sicily to the Rome of Rossellini and Fellini. When, years later, Toto returns to his hometown for the projectionist's funeral (the only thing powerful enough to draw him back), the cinema stands derelict. He gains access to the building and recalls its heyday as the centre of social life. As he witnesses the building's demolition, surrounded by the now wizened and aged figures who defined his youth, he watches the social world of the cinema give way to the private world as expressed through TV, video and the cocoon of the car – the cinema is to be demolished to make way for a car park. Of course, it is all a little too convenient – that the cinema should be demolished exactly when Toto (now Salvatore) returns, for instance – but it is all symbolic, allegorical rather than real.

The cinema spans a period which saw huge migration from the country to the city, from the turn of the century to the depressed years following the Second World War. The high point of the cinema came during this period of radical transition. In terms of attendance and the building of cinemas, this was the defining period. It could be said that the cinema began to replace the church as the social and ritual centre of the urban fabric. Friday and Saturday night at the movies, and Saturday morning for the kids, became institutions as ingrained as Sunday morning at Mass or other days of religious observance.

For the masses who made the harsh transition to urban poverty in hopeful search of relief from the grind of rural subsistence, the cinema became a place of escape. The church promised redemption and reward in the afterlife; the cinema offered more immediate relief. Like the church building, the cinema building became an architectural hoarding, expressing the sublimity of another realm – Heaven or Hollywood must have seemed virtually interchangeable. But Hollywood was more attainable; the cinema became a more real and more tangible centre than the church.

The concept of the cinema as a kind of modern version of the church in a faithless society, or at least a society where celebrity and glamour are what is worshipped and greedily consumed, is an intriguing one. When the Gothic masons built their finest cathedrals, the aim was to create an architecture of light. The walls would melt away into nothing to reveal the drama and the power of the light from the heavens refracted and reflected through the myriad fragments of stained glass. Cinemas are every bit as much buildings about light, yet it is a purely artificial light. Thus they appear as blind boxes, desperate to keep the light from getting in – if anything they emanate a heavenly glow in an effort to convert the unconverted. It was this idea which led to the German innovation of *Lichtarchitektur*, where the cinema exudes light, expressing its interior function as well as advertising itself and introducing the kind of tower (read spire) more normally associated with the position of a church in a landscape.

Tornatore is quite explicit in this religious analogy; we first see Toto as altar boy. The mysteries of the Mass do not hold him in thrall, quite the opposite; he falls asleep and forgets to ring the communion bell as the Host is raised – too many late nights at the movies. The rituals of the Church cannot compete with the more visceral delights and the mystery and romance of film. In fact the movies become a symbol for love: the kissing scenes cut out by the zealous priest (who indicates his displeasure by ringing the same communion bell), and never returned by the projectionist to the distributor, stand in place of Toto's failed romance, and it is this that makes the ending – a rush through the history of film embraces – so poignant. Of course, the cinema also becomes the backdrop for the illicit romances of the small town – it begins to represent a kind of venality, which is precisely what the priest fears. But it is this sense of the cinema as a place of love, of fantasy and escape, of relief from monotony or poverty, which Tornatore brings to life so magically in *Cinema Paradiso*.

The idea of the cinema as a place of relief from the strict moral codes of a community that brought the conservative morality of the countryside to the town is remarkably powerful in film. The darkness of the auditorium provided the perfect cover for teenage sexual fumblings, for illicit encounters and more grown-up gropings. Barry Levinson's nostalgic 1982 film *Diner* (a film to put girls off popcorn), as well as countless other teen-flicks and coming-of-age films, feature movie theatres at the heart of teenage sexual awakening. The drive-in, with the accompanying privacy of the automobile interior, lent a whole new impetus to the notion of the movies as a place of coupling.

During the late 1960s and 1970s, a far less innocent vision of the cinema as the site of sexual liaisons emerged. As TV pushed film aside, theatre owners began to look for new markets and, in the days before porn was made readily available by home video systems, sex films became a staple of struggling urban cinemas, guaranteeing an audience which would pay over the odds to see films which could not be seen elsewhere. When Toto returns to the remains of the Cinema Paradiso, the posters he sees are for cheesy 1970s sex films, the last gasp of the small-town cinema. In film this transformation of the cinema into a pit of urban degradation is eloquently shown in scenes from two seminal films: Martin Scorsese's *Taxi Driver* (1976) and John Schlesinger's *Midnight Cowboy* (1969).

In both films, the seedy underbelly of New York is expressed through scenes in porn cinemas. In *Taxi Driver*, Travis Bickle, the eponymous psychotic loner, watches a sex film in a manner both curious and detached and then takes his date to a porno movie. In *Midnight Cowboy* the central character reaches his nadir as he is reduced to selling his body after his naive

Cinema Paradiso

Poster for The Man with a Movie Camera

dreams of becoming a kept man have disintegrated. These scenes reveal not only the darker nature of the city but also the decline of the cinema itself. From the dream palace of the 1930s, the movie theatre metamorphoses into a wet-dream booth for the 1970s.

While Scorsese and Schlesinger portray the seamy side of the big city using images of the cinema, Peter Bogdanovich's *The Last Picture Show* (1971) uses the cinema as a metaphor for the decline of small-town life. The film begins and ends with the image of the decrepit little tumbledown movie theatre. When the theatre's charismatic owner dies, the cinema dies with him, a slow death which echoes the familiar drudgery of Nowheresville, USA. The old Westerns that play at the cinema seem to reflect the chasm between the frontier mentality of the cowboys and the ennui of the small Texas towns they left in their wake. There is little of the romanticised escapism which enthuses Toto to become a film-maker in *Cinema Paradiso*. Rather the theatre in *The Last Picture Show* evokes an air of desperate boredom, the last semblance of entertainment in a town where there's nothing to do and no one new to meet. It is a kind of antidote to the saccharine, life-affirming picture of small-town US life seen in Frank Capra's *It's a Wonderful Life* (1946).

The cinema building as a filmic motif seems to recur again and again as a metaphor for decline, for the passing of a gentler, kinder world. In *The Smallest Show on Earth* (1957), a young couple inherit a dilapidated cinema from an eccentric relation. The building comes with a full complement of senile staff and the whole operation is run as a kind of community project. This is contrasted with the corporate predator who is trying to buy out the little theatre to demolish it and establish an entertainment monopoly. It is an affectionate view of the cinema as the centre of the community, very much like the Cinema Paradiso.

The figure of the kindly, avuncular projectionist pops up in another film, which uses the image of the cinema in a very different way. *The Last Action Hero* (1993), a hugely expensive, would-be blockbuster which spectacularly failed to bust blocks, featured just such a projectionist who becomes the guide to a film-loving little boy who finds a magic ticket which allows him to interact with the movies and characters on the screen – Schwarzenegger et al. This is an odd, and occasionally (surprisingly) interesting film which blends elements from the *Cinema Paradiso* notion of the movie theatre as place of escape with the more literal idea of the cinema as gateway to another world.

We are all familiar with the story of the early film (1896 in fact) showing a train moving towards the camera which shocked the audience into fleeing the auditorium in fear of their lives. Thus we can see that the idea of the world of film crossing into the physical world of the cinema is one that has fascinated film-makers and audiences for as long as there has been film. Buster Keaton's *Sherlock Junior* (1924), perhaps the best film to exploit this idea, features the director as a cinema employee who falls asleep and makes the transition through the screen into the glamorous world of the movies.

The motif of a protagonist in a film reaching out to a member of the audience (usually an actor who has been hired to interact with the film using rehearsed lines) is another familiar technique often used to break down the barrier of the screen. In a similar way, film actors have appropriated theatrical conventions asides and glances askew at the audience (think of Oliver Hardy's pained expression as he is exasperated beyond words by another of Stan Laurel's near balletic feats of clumsiness, or of Woody Allen's chats to camera in innumerable films). All these devices begin to blur the divisions between the audience and what, in the theatre, would be the space behind the proscenium arch, which in the movie theatre is only suggested by the illusion of depth of the film.

Soviet directors were among the first to question profoundly the role of the medium and to make audiences aware of their role as spectators. Dziga Vertov was a part of the early Soviet agitprop cinema and travelled around the country on trains compiling footage of the civil war and of the far corners of the country. His later work would always be informed by his beginnings as a documentary and propaganda film-maker and his work can be seen as a concerted attack on the very idea of narrative and fiction in film. His development of the idea of *Kino-Pravda* (Cine-truth) was later echoed during the 1960s French move towards *cinéma-vérité*. In *A Sixth Part of the World* (1926), a masterful Soviet propaganda film revelling in the scale of the Russian motherland, the audience is jolted out of their status as unthinking spectators by sporadic shots of an on-screen audience watching scenes from the film itself.

Vertov was determined to instil an objective, rational detachment in his audience. He reached the pinnacle of his efforts in *The Man with a Movie Camera* (1929), a complex, confusing but constantly striking work, which is essentially a film about making and watching film. A stream of pictures of cameras are juxtaposed and superimposed on mechanistic images, lenses and eyes, while an empty cinema auditorium is intermittently shown filling up. The audience is constantly made aware of its own spectatorship and of the mechanics of film-making, projection and vision. Reflecting on editing, the film bombards the audience with confusing layers of images and action, often with no apparent effort at continuity and negating the possibility of comprehension. Vertov silently makes a point about the trickery of the editor in a stream of images which has perhaps never been surpassed in its originality or visual dynamism. After film-making and editing, Vertov brings the audience's attention back to itself with a section of the film that deals with ideas of viewing, feeding the spectators images of another audience staring back at them.

What Vertov does is to subvert the idea that the screen is a magical dimension, that there is a mystical depth behind the hint of a proscenium arch. He brings the audience back down to earth by reminding it of its presence and of the manipulation of the directors, cameramen and editors. The cinema space, the auditorium, becomes a place of potential deception. While the capitalist world was erecting dream palaces, Vertov was opening eyes to the reality of life, to the hardships of working people throughout the vast Soviet territories. The cinema becomes a place not of escape but of engagement with political reality. The film was made at the time that the most lavish super-cinemas and exotic theatres were being erected in the USA and Europe. It is the portrayal of the diametric opposite of the very conception of those picture palaces.

Vertov was not only ahead of his time – the sophistication of his work has remained unsurpassed. The images of the screen and the cinema building have continued to be used to portray the kind of place of transformation which Vertov tried so hard to dismiss. The flat screen becomes more akin to an opening to another world. The cinema becomes an interactive building, the action on screen reflected in the reaction of the audience. Tears, screams, tightly gripped boyfriends and husbands, uproarious laughter; the cinema is a cathartic space in a way which is hard to understand when you are confronted by an empty auditorium. The emptiness means that the cinema can become a cipher for almost any mood, memory or dream.

In *Annie Hall* Woody Allen uses the motif of the cinema as an intellectual haven, the modern cultural replacement of the Central European café, a venue for angst and a kind of self-imposed suffering. He seems to go to the movies not to enjoy himself, but to impose Bergman, or

whoever, upon himself. Of course we know that Allen enjoys Bergman's bleak films, but he is conscious of their depressive effect. He is a man who likes to be depressed. It is a very different image of cinema from that in *Cinema Paradiso*, but equally central to a way of life.

In John Landis's *An American Werewolf in London* (1981), the cinema becomes a venue for transformation as the central character metamorphoses into a monster. Countless other horror flicks use the same imagery, which essentially builds on a blend of *The Phantom of the Opera* and the Hammer Horror tradition. Tim Burton's *Ed Wood* plays on horror traditions using the genre's worst director as a vehicle. The film both begins and ends in a cinema. At the start we see the almost empty cinema on press night. A space meant for a crowd can look forlornly lonely without one and the loneliness of Wood's epic struggle is framed from the beginning. The film's happy (or as happy as could be in Wood's tragic circumstances) ending witnesses another premiere and Wood leaves with his wife-to-be before the audience has time to react to the awfulness of *Plan 9 from Outer Space*, the worst film ever made. Burton's final shot is a kind of tongue-in-cheek tribute to Hollywood, as the camera flies high over the neons of the Pantages Theater and reveals the Hollywood Hills and the famous Hollywood sign beyond. The cinema becomes a kind of neon-lit gateway in this beautiful, nostalgic shot, a gateway to the wonderful world of glamour and the movies, a land from which the hapless Wood will remain excluded. The cinema building itself excludes him, just as all the studios do beyond.

In gangster and crime films, the cinema is often used as a place of refuge, a dark, crowded haven where the quarry goes to lie low from pursuers, presenting another interesting twist on the cinema/church analogy. *Dillinger* (1945, second time around 1973) is undoubtedly the most famous of this genre, although the sanctuary of the cinema is not respected by the police, who gun the robber down outside its doors in one of the most memorable uses of the cinema on screen.

The cinema is undoubtedly a sacred space, a space of ritual, of magic and of transformation and it is this image which movie-makers have been using for over a century. To return to *Cinema Paradiso*, the symbol of the cinema is the sculpted lion's head that frames the light from the projector. The lion's head, whether Tornatore knew it or not, is the traditional symbol of the sun, of light. The mythical status of the cinema is nowhere more revered than on the screen, despite the efforts of Vertov and his man with a movie camera.

***IMAX**, Waterloo, London*

AVERY ASSOCIATES

The cylindrical form of Avery Associates' London IMAX cinema (1999) is dictated by its site – a grim hole in the centre of a polluted and traffic-clogged roundabout just beyond London's South Bank arts complex. The site was formerly a kind of urban black hole, a concrete pit with confusing, dark subways spouting off in all directions – one of London's least attractive spots. In a scheme which has a significant regenerative brief, the architects have attempted to replace the hole with a hub, a lively building which brings colour and movement to the hitherto determinedly pedestrian-unfriendly approach to Waterloo Bridge. As the building went up, it looked at times a little cold and mechanical, but now it is complete London's largest IMAX cinema looks like the best, in fact almost the only, solution to this awkward site.

Clad in a glazed curtain wall, the structure is deliberately lightweight in appearance as an antidote to the grim stained concrete and grimy brick which characterise the area. Its perfect cylindrical form seems to suggest the all-encompassing nature of the entertainment within – a billboard for the IMAX medium itself. The glazed drum surrounds a solid core, but the mass of the building is reduced by a painting which wraps itself right the way around the drum. Garishly colourful and striking, the enormous abstract image is the work of Howard Hodgkin. The largest piece of public art in London, it is one of the very few examples of fine art presented truly democratically – from both sides of the river, in traffic, on a bus or anywhere around Waterloo, there is no escaping it; this really is art for the people.

Seen from above, with its shallow saucer-like dome, its delicate metalwork struts which support the glazing, and with Hodgkin's splashes of colour, the building takes on an almost fairground feel. Reminiscent of a great merry-go-round at the centre of the roundabout, it recalls the early days of cinema as fairground entertainment – a mesmerising and mysterious booth. There is something appropriate about this analogy as the IMAX is often presented as an educational tool, with IMAX screens appearing all over the world in museums and science parks; the lurid splash of Avery's drum brings the IMAX back into the fold of the popular and the urban.

The interior is cool and High-Tech, occasionally reminiscent of Avery's earlier Museum of the Moving Image, which used to sit nearby beneath a grim concrete platform. Here too, Avery had succeeded in producing a lively and popular set of spaces from a dismal and unpromising setting through the use of a profusion of High-Tech detailing and glass. The entrance sequence of the IMAX is dominated by a grand staircase, a tradition that seems to have been revived from the early history of cinema architecture when theatrical conventions held more weight. The high point of this sequence, however, comes when entering the auditorium. Rather than following the normal custom of locating access at the rear of the theatre, the architects engineered an arrival at the foot of the cinema's huge single screen. The immense screen that makes the IMAX such an attraction immediately looms over visitors and impresses upon them the scale of the building and the forthcoming experience.

Hodgkin's blown-up painting is not the only specially commissioned work to liven up this dismal roundabout. The profoundly unattractive subways around the site have all received some kind of aesthetic treatment, the best being a constellation of tiny lights against a blue background. The ring of circulation around the cinema has been crowned with a halo of hanging plants and greenery to help distance it from its polluted environment. The subways remain unappealing but the new cinema has lifted the area immensely.

IMAX, Waterloo, London

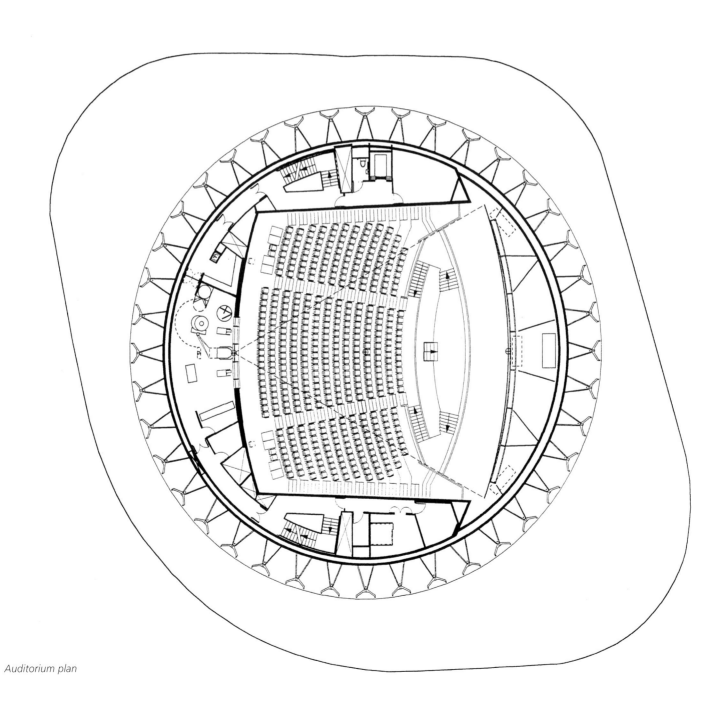

Auditorium plan

BELOW: *Cross section showing the proximity of the Underground*

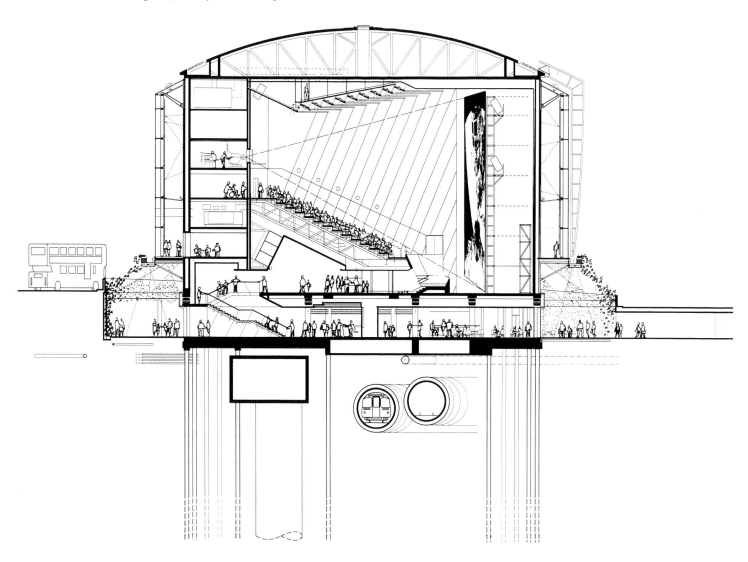

BEHNISCH, BEHNISCH AND PARTNER

During the 1960s, when Europe's city centres were filling up with overscaled speculative office developments, the cinema as a separate building type virtually died. London and Paris in particular saw new cinemas subsumed into vast, characterless blocks, with only meagre illuminated signs poking out at street level to betray the presence of entertainment. These new cinemas tended to be as oppressive and bland as the lumpen buildings into which they were squeezed. The problem was that in functionalist terms the cinema is a difficult building to express architecturally. Burying auditoria in office developments was seen as an easy way out of actually having to design a cinema, while also making a profitable use of city-centre sites.

When Behnisch, Behnisch and Partner came to design a large banking services centre for the Landesgirokasse in Stuttgart, Germany, they decided to reduce the traditional deadening impact on the streetscape of such a huge office development by engaging with the public realm. German city centres are prone to a glut of office developments which tend to leave the hearts of the great cities dead in the evenings. The cinema built as part of this complex has been used as the vehicle to create a zone between the ostensibly private space of the offices and the public realm of the surrounding streets and squares. Conceived only late in the project, the cinema had to be slotted into leftover space whilst also becoming an integral part of the overall scheme. This was achieved by breaking down the solidity of the barriers between the street and the cinema. The elevation to the street is completely glazed and can be opened during the summer months. Brightly lit, dazzling colours create an enticingly warm public foyer, contrasting with the more austere steel and glass expression of the administrative parts of the bank on the upper levels.

Kino Atelier am Bollwerk, *Stuttgart*

The cinema, Atelier am Bollwerk (1997), consists of three studio-size auditoria, each with an individual character, differentiated by varying the patterns of wall panels. Dedicated to art-house and independent movies, it is designed as a deliberate urban counterpoint to the large out-of-town cinemas showing popular blockbusters. The real, commercial money-making is confined to the sprawling bank above.

The other scheme featured here is a design for a movie palace at the Olympiapark in Munich (1990) which, unfortunately, was never realised.

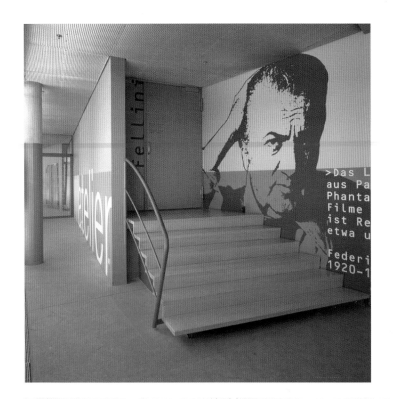

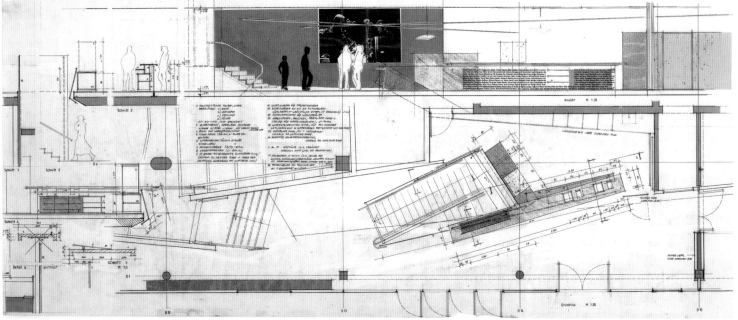
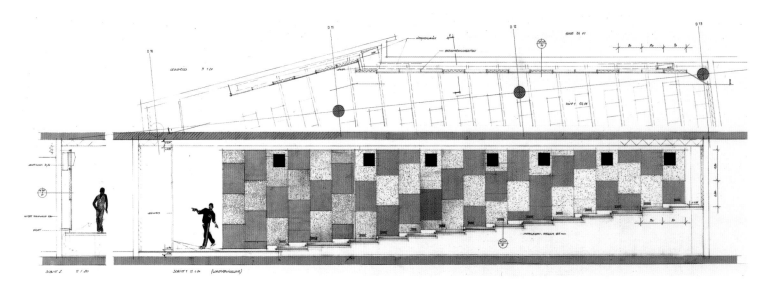

Plan and section drawings of lobby area

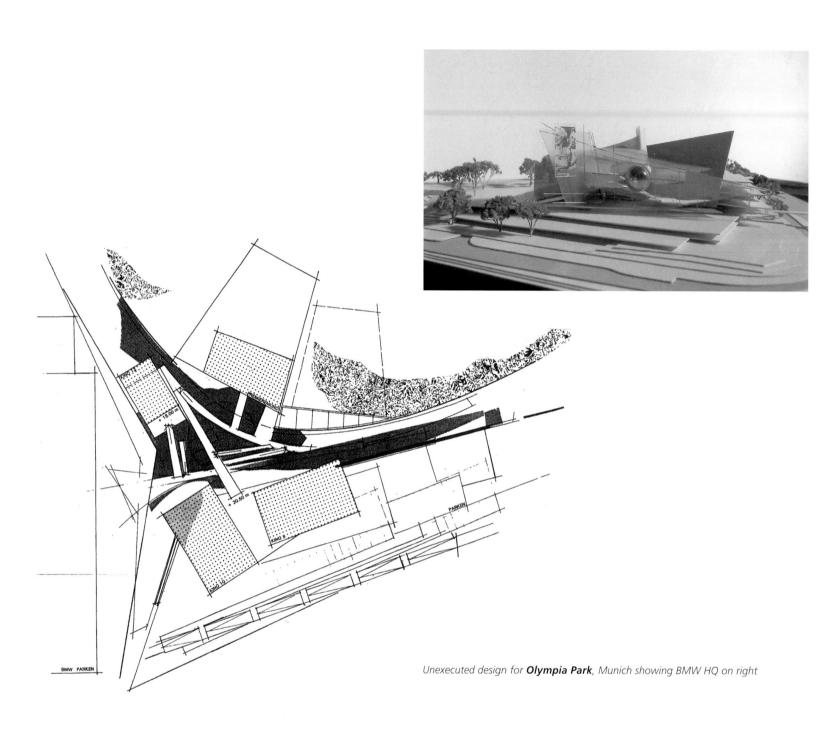

*Unexecuted design for **Olympia Park**, Munich showing BMW HQ on right*

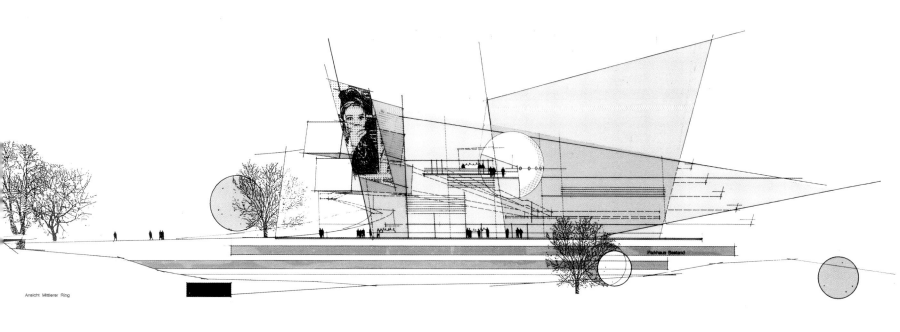

Ansicht Mittlerer Ring

Parkhaus Bestand

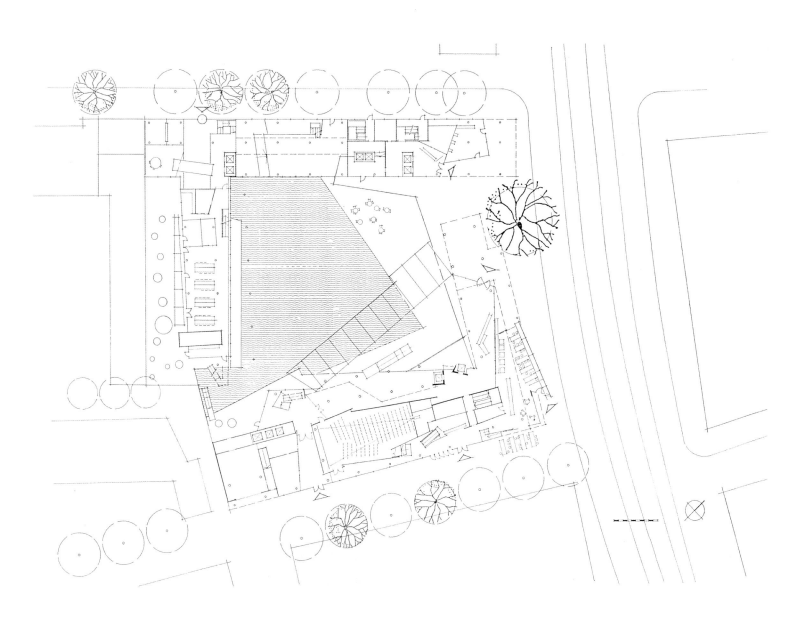

BURRELL FOLEY FISCHER

One of the first offices to re-examine the architecture of the urban cinema in the 1990s was the British practice Burrell Foley Fischer. The last two decades of the twentieth century in Britain, as elsewhere, had been dominated by the out-of-town complex – effectively a shed with a group of screens crammed in as close as possible, surrounded by an infinite car park. The Harbour Lights Cinema in Southampton (1995) was one of the earliest reactions to this deadening architectural *oeuvre* and it remains among the most striking and sculptural cinemas of recent years.

The inspiration for this dock-side building is unmissable – like a ship about to be launched, its presence is announced by a dramatic prow leaning longingly towards the water. The timber-clad sides of this cantilevered prow seem to refer back to the ancient boat-building tradition of the docks. Cutting through the prow element, the sleek, glazed structure which houses the stairs recalls the nautical streamlining of the 1930s, the heyday of the cruise liner and the last great period of these docks. The jutting prow has been formed by continuing the line

Harbour Lights Cinema, *Southampton*

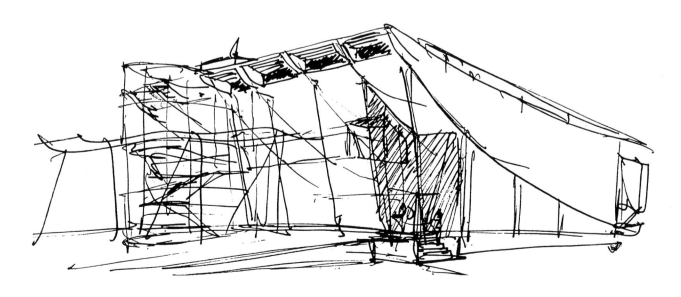

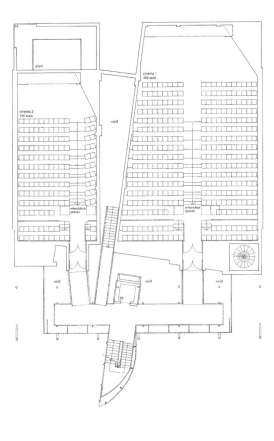

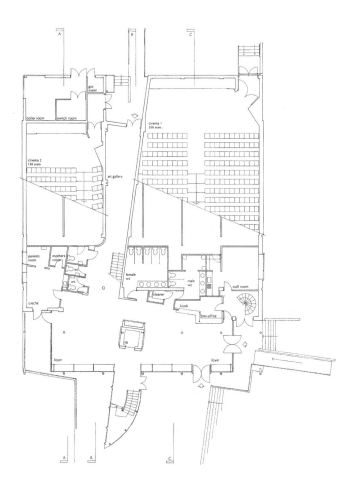

of the rake of the seating beyond the auditorium until it meets the roof at a strikingly sharp point like the end of a carving knife. The glass blade of the stairwell bisects the building and creates a circulation zone between the two auditoria, reappearing on the other side of the building as a fissure at its centre. Terraces and a great deal of transparency make the most of the dockside position and open the building out to the sea, while the slanted glazing of the lobby recalls the shape of a ship's bridge.

The Stratford Picture House (1997) in East London is similarly transparent and has played an important part in regenerating a deprived and often physically incoherent part of the city, scarred by busy roads and rail lines and by poor design. The public parts of the building aim to enliven an area which has been designated a 'cultural quarter' and which includes a turn-of-the-century theatre.

A long, glazed lobby addresses the public realm outside, completely opening out the building. The glazed curtain wall is slightly set back beneath a canopy, which is supported by a row of spindly columns, tying the elements of the main elevation together. Beyond the lobby a long, gently curving wall unifies the entrances to the four cinemas, which increase in size from one side to the other. The volumes of the separate auditoria are all individually expressed on the rear of the building in a stepped wall which follows the line of the street. The short section through the building shows how closely the envelope follows the forms of the internal spaces. The sectional shape of the bar echoes the sloping roof of the auditoria, which itself responds to the beams of the projector, while the skewed stair between lobby and cinemas reflects the steep rake of the seating. The continuous curved wall enclosing the single projection room (more accurately described as a projection corridor in which all projectors can be operated by one projectionist) encroaches into the foyer, the walls of which seem to react by leaning back to give themselves breathing room. A slanting, continuous rooflight compounds the skewed appearance of this dynamic and complex circulation space.

Harbour Lights, plans

It is an unusual and interesting case of the technical aspects of the film process exerting an influence on the public spaces. The impact of the machinery on the building form can be seen again in the crest of the building, which is formed by a plant gantry enclosed in an industrial mesh structure. The functionalist notion of the built elements expressing their purpose has rarely been realised in a cinema and it is fascinating to see one where the external form has been extruded from its internal workings.

The Lux Cinema in Hoxton, East London (1997), represents an altogether different approach for a tighter, more urban site in a typical London square with gardens at its centre. The Lux is set within a starkly simple building (designed by MacCreanor Lavington) in which the frame is expressed in a subdued grey-brick grid, a reflection of the functional industrial architecture and warehouses which characterise the area. As in Burrell Foley Fischer's other cinemas, the lobby is opened out to the public realm with a fully glazed street frontage which leads to a light lobby enlivened by a series of moving images and glass insertions in the floor. The lobby lends a sense of movement and of the flickering light of the screen to the public realm while the transition between the square and the lobby is seamless and fluid. Subtle and understated, it is a very fine urban intervention.

Stratford Picture House, *East London*

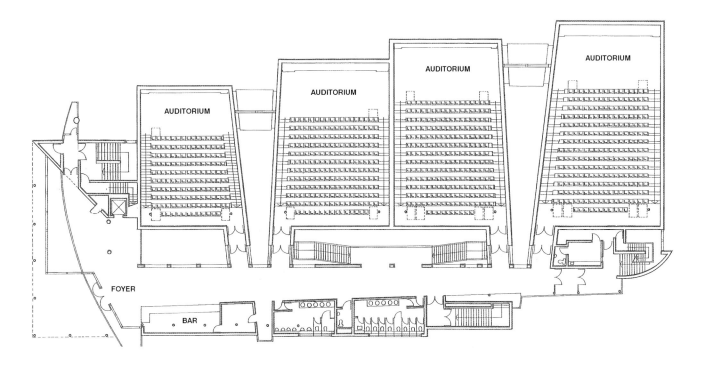

LUX Cinema, *Hoxton, East London*

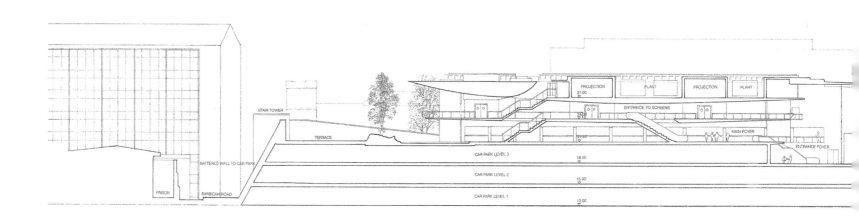

Blackfriar Multiplex, *Gloucester, Section*

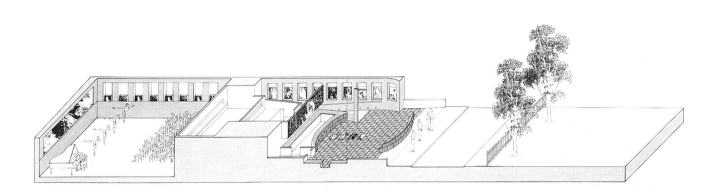

LUX Cinema, Hoxton, East London, Model

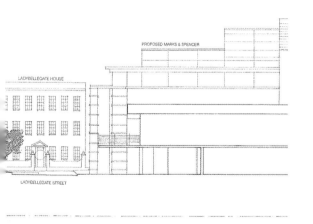

Blackfriars Multiplex, Gloucester, Model

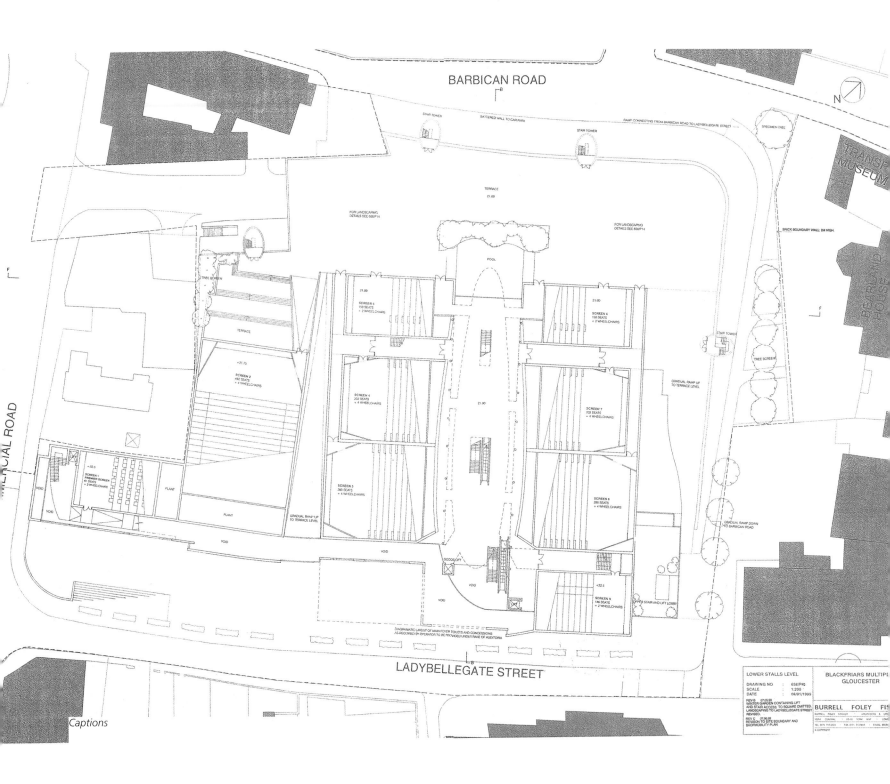

BARBICAN ROAD

LADYBELLEGATE STREET

Captions

Blackfriar Multiplex, Gloucester, Plan

METRO, *auditorium, isometric*

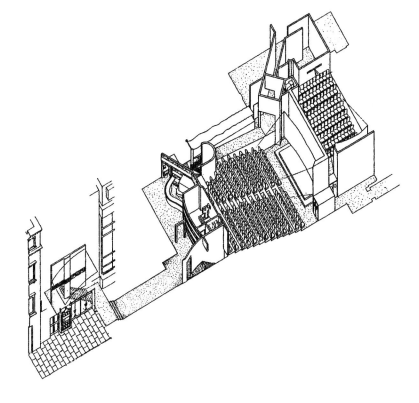

RIO, *auditorium*

Harkins Superstition Springs

CCBG ARCHITECTS

Set into the harsh desert landscape of Arizona, the rich colours of the Superstition Springs (1998) glow under the permanently blue sky. The cinema, built for Harkins Theatres, is a twenty-five screen megaplex which makes little effort to hide its spreading mass or the essential simplicity of its functional, low-budget design. This utilitarian approach, combined with a sculptural composition of simple planes and purely expressed functional elements, typifies the approach to cinema design of American architects CCBG. A tilted grid supports both lettering and a squiggly neon composition but also completes and defines a forecourt in front of the expansive glass elevation. A long canopy introduces a human scale to the vast complex and allows for slightly more comfortable queuing or waiting in the unforgiving desert conditions. The lobby is bound by a glass curtain wall with integral aluminium shades which create a sculptural element within the otherwise simple elevations. The shades, together with a deeply cantilevered roof, assist in sheltering the lobby area from the blistering Arizona sun, yet allow for a huge expanse of glazing so that the interior remains fully visible from without. A canary-yellow concrete plane penetrates the glazed wall and emphasises the continuity of the forecourt area and the lobby as a single public space.

Harkins Superstition Springs

Harkins Superstition Springs

The same essential strategy is employed at CCBG's other cinema buildings for Harkins Theatres. This approach consists of a large, partially enclosed forecourt and a heavily glazed, dramatically lit lobby space. The Flagstaff 11, Arizona, was inspired, according to the architects, by the massing of the vintage highway hotels in the desert into complexes which are highly visible from the road and become freeway landmarks. A huge curtain wall allows a clear view into an active, powerfully vertical lobby which is enlivened by a three-dimensional arrangement of abstract neons. The smooth, continuous surfaces of the elevations give way inside to a much more complex arrangement of masses and planes, although the glass wall always allows referral back to the deep, piercing blue of the Arizona sky.

The Arizona Mills 24 is a much larger megaplex, similar in size to Superstition Springs 25 (which has twent-five screens to the twenty-four of Arizona Mills). A screen structure helps to enclose a sheltered forecourt as well as bearing the corporate lettering and giving the cinema element of the building an identity distinct from the mall in which it is placed. A series of simple, blocky masses behind this screen is articulated by repetitive abstract patterns formed by variations in the cladding. But there is little to hide the unabashed functionalism of the cinema – this is stripped-down warehouse architecture to house blind boxes. Only a few intersecting planes embellished in bright colours relieve the repetitiveness of the long, low-lying walls. The lobby is a different matter altogether. The high-ceilinged space is punctuated by a series of angular neons and tilted screens which fills the huge volume of the space with a three-dimensional light sculpture.

Harkings Flagstaff II

Arizona Mills 24

Modernissimo, *Naples*

CDS ARCHITETTI ASSOCIATI

CDS seem to treat cinema buildings like abstract art works. Each design becomes a three-dimensional canvas, an explosion of colour and form varying wildly in feel, scale and texture from one building to another, vibrantly individualistic yet clearly recognisable. This treatment of the building as an abstract composition is shown most clearly in images of design proposals: planes are treated as colour blocks in the vein of De Stijl; boldly sculpted interiors display disco glitter or sleek metallic surfaces.

Ignoring the usual route to success – the development of a single house style – CDS have been producing a fantastic range of extraordinarily varied yet consistently intriguing buildings, which have received relatively little media coverage outside Italy. The Modernissimo in Naples (1993) has proved to be one of their most enduringly interesting schemes. A remodelling of an existing building, the project saw an uninteresting structure turned into a thoughtful and elegant piece of Modernism, combining elements of De Stijl and classic early functionalist design with richly sculptural spatial transformations. The facade to the street has the appearance of unreconstructed functionalism – ribbon windows and white walls all supported on black *piloti*. Yet the interior, visible through the transparent floor, reveals a clash of planes in vibrant primary colours. The effect is toned down for the self-consciously monotone bar (moodily grey/blue with only hints of colour) yet is revived in the unusual auditoria. The main auditorium is enriched by the billowing underbelly of the projection room which creates a dramatic ceiling and allows the space to expand rapidly towards the screen.

The success of this scheme led to another Modernissimo, this time in Salerno (1995). Here the colourful planes and the bright red that has become characteristic of the work of CDS are taken through to the elevations via the building's cladding, which enlivens an otherwise unspectacular streetscape. In the sleek and functional auditorium, bright red defines a frame around the screen, a memory of the proscenium arch. Again, the subtly curving ceiling introduces a dynamic, pushing the emphasis of the space inexorably towards the glare of the screen.

Modernissimo, *Naples*

Modernissimo, Salerno

A stronger hint of the powerful memory of the proscenium can be seen in the designs for the Felix Cinema in Chiaiano (1998). A bold, red frame curves and wraps around the screen and echoes the omnipresent brilliant red of the lobbies. The brightly coloured lines of the kitsch interior recall a kind of 1960s sci-fi aesthetic, an image reinforced by the mirrored ceiling, which distorts audiences into wobbly images tinged with the reflected pinky-red light bouncing off the walls.

In the wake of the success of the Modernissimo cinemas, CDS launched into a prolific phase which saw them building an incredible array of different cinemas. The bright colours in the auditorium at the Alcione in Naples (1998) lead the eye around a thoughtfully sculptural space given an almost theatrical form by a gallery and stair. The odd Duel Cinema in Pozzuoli (1999) delights in the contrast between the warehouse aesthetic of the forecourt,

Felix Cinema, *Chiaiano*

TOP LEFT: **Felix Cinema**, *Chiaiano*
TOP RIGHT: **Alcione Cinema**, *Naples*
BOTTOM: **Duel Cinema**, *Pozzuoli*

the elevations and the rusty trusses of the auditoria ceilings on the one hand and, on the other hand, the disco-glitter foyer with silver-spangled columns and a jokey retro feel. The focus of attention at La Perla cinema in Naples (1999) is firmly fixed on the UFO-shaped saucers which crowd the ceiling of the auditorium.

The stream of cinemas gushing from the office is unceasing and includes a number of potentially fascinating schemes. The pared-down Modernism of the subtle Tito Cinema (Potenza), and the clean, functional lines of the more monumental Nonsolo Cinema (Caserta) present an intriguing alternative to the usual out-of-town boxes. The sculptural, heavily modelled forms of the Ponticelli and Mediterraneo (both in Naples) and the Marcianise (Caserta) express the disposition of the internal elements of the building, and the auditoria in particular, to produce a recognisable architectural language of the cinema based on massing and volume. A similar approach has been attempted at the Afragola, only here the purity of the building's internal volumes has been broken down by a series of wildly colourful interpenetrating planes so that, just as at the Modernissimo cinemas, the architects create an abstract work of art from the prosaic elements of the building.

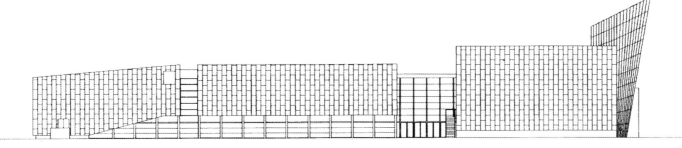

Tito, *Potenza*

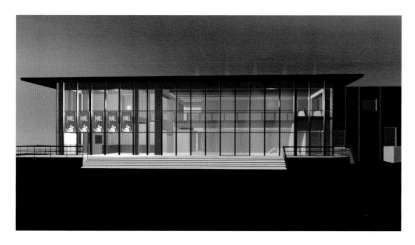

Nonsolocinema, *design*

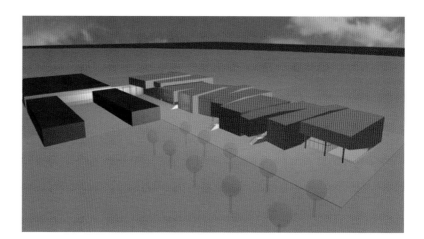

Ponticelli, *design*

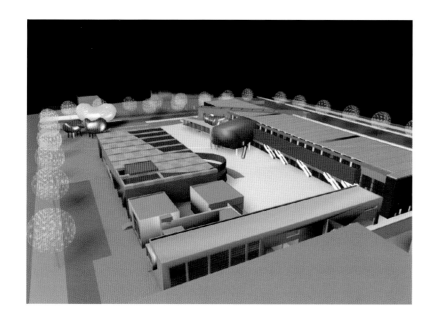

Marcianese, *design*

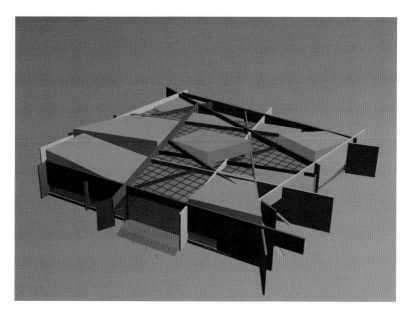

Afragola, *design*

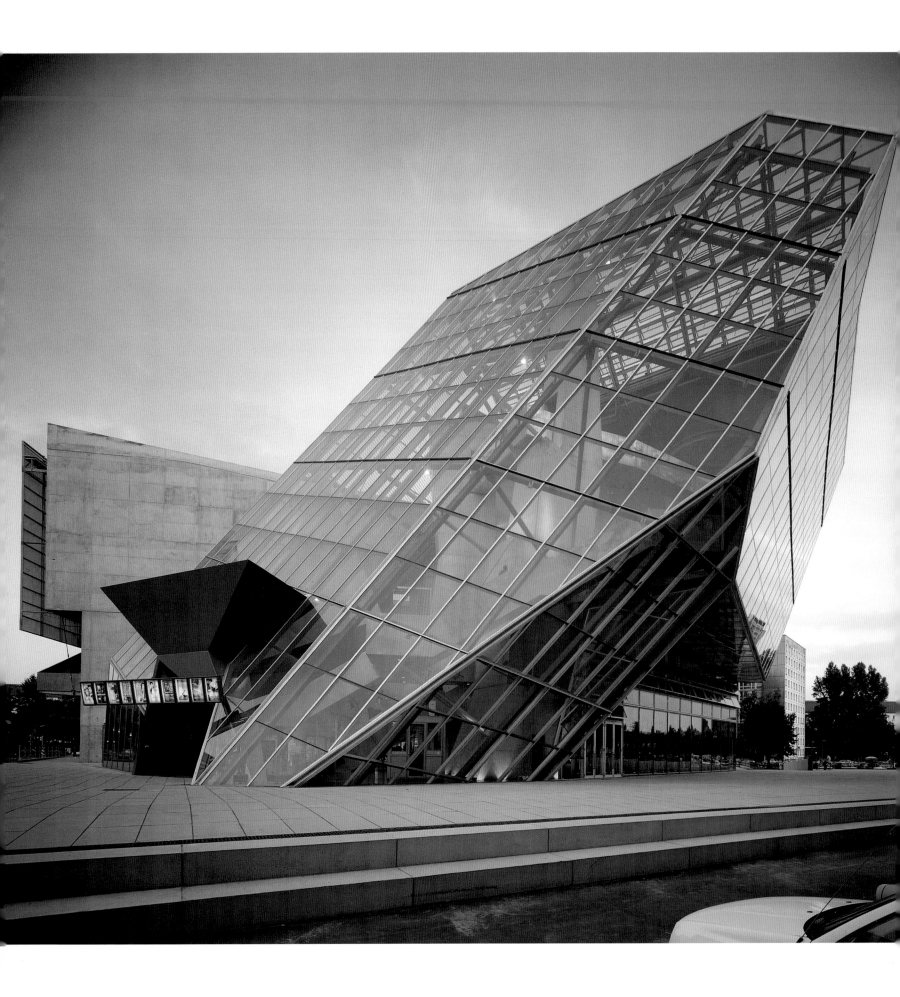

COOP HIMMELB(L)AU

Cinema architects have very rarely been able to match the potential of film to fragment time and collapse space into infinitely varied narratives. Coop Himmelb(l)au's UFA Palast in Dresden (1993–98) is the only cinema building of recent years to have begun to deconstruct space and architectural narrative in a manner directly inspired by film. The jarring angles and jagged shadows cast on the concrete walls recall the psycho-spaces of Expressionist film and early German attempts to infuse architecture with as much motion, emotion and uncertainty as could be conveyed by the medium itself.

Whereas traditional theatres suggest an architectural form with an auditorium wrapping around a stage, a

flytower and front and back of house facilities, the cinema presents only the blind box. The architectural content tends to be wrapped around the solid core of the auditorium as an insulated, dumb volume. The fantastic forms of the UFA Palast, perhaps surprisingly, are also created in this way. The cinemas are arranged over three storeys in a solid concrete spine anchoring the building down on one side while the dramatically fragmented glass structures of the circulation and public parts of the building cascade down the other side. By encasing so much of the building in glass the architects have managed to reduce the mass of a huge multiplex and its effect on the townscape. Rather than presenting a monolithic block spread over a large floor

UFA Palast, *Dresden, plans*

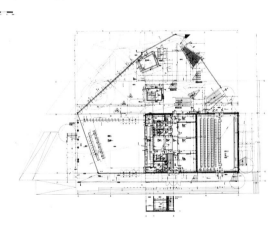

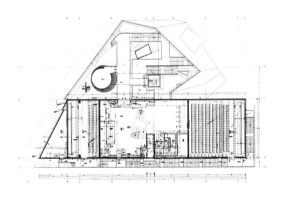

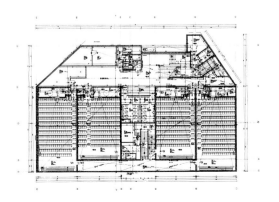

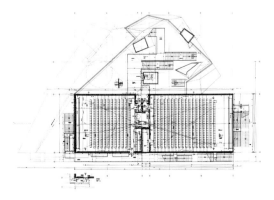

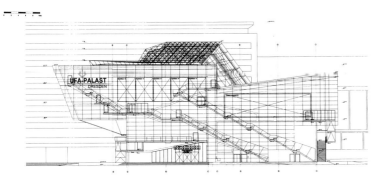

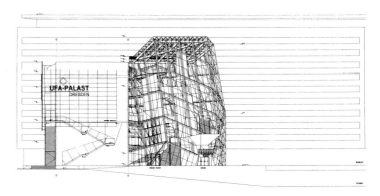

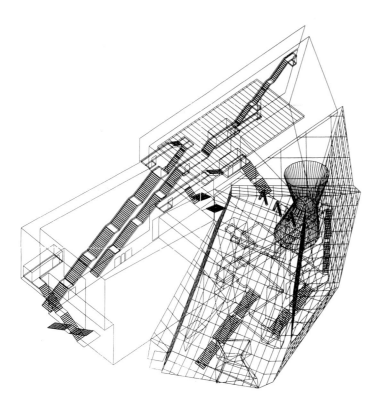

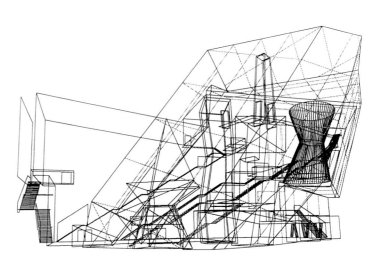

UFA Palast *elevations, isometric and section*

area consequently killing off a large section of the city, Coop Himmelb(l)au have piled up the cinema centre into a sculptural mass which both defines and creates a public space. In common with Koen van Velsen's Rotterdam Pathe Cinema, the UFA Palast is wrapped around an enclosed public space which aims to integrate the cinema into the network of circulation patterns of the city itself. Unlike so many cinemas which are vibrant only once the visitor is inside, the UFA Palast presents a transparent front and the dramatic internal spaces become part of a complex urban game. At night in particular, the building becomes a cystalline lamp displaying a series of complex and fragmented images to the city in a

reflection of the vibrancy of the cinema screens within. One wall of the building, a great cliff of concrete diagonally bisected by stairs climbing up the facade, becomes a huge screen for the showing of trailers so that the static building becomes a foil for images and movement which feed the motion of the city.

The huge surfaces of glass and concrete could have become an alienating mass reducing humans to an ant-like ineffectuality, but this problem of scale has been redressed by the insertion of a number of sculptural elements which reintroduce a human scale while defining specific areas within the vast volumes of the public spaces. The most distinctive of these internal structures is the waisted metal cage which sits over a

circular platform. This little terrace which sits suspended in an atrium at the heart of the structure supports a few tables and chairs belonging to the café and serves as a vantage point. It also introduces a kind of James Bond villain's-lair aesthetic which seems to perfectly suit the film-set drama of this sculptural interior. Bridges and stairs slicing through the spaces at theatrical angles and a crumpled-looking elevator tower also help to bring a human scale to the monumental atrium. The short cross-section through the building best describes the drama of this glass hall and its fragmentation by the series of elements placed within it. It also powerfully recalls the notion of the glass mountain which pervaded so much of German

Expressionist visionary architecture. In these visions (notably in the early designs of Hans Scharoun, Bruno and Max Taut and the Czech, Wenzel Hablik) the crystalline building was seen as radiating a divine light, a kind of earth energy. Here those rays of light seem to be transformed into the beams from the projector, in the way in which the building emanates a glow illuminating the surrounding streets. The contrast of the lightness and sparkling brilliance of the huge walls of glass and the heavy concrete structures containing the auditoria which anchor the building to the earth reinforce this notion of the revival of Expressionist imagery, of the building as a crystal cathedral rising mystically from the solid rock of the earth.

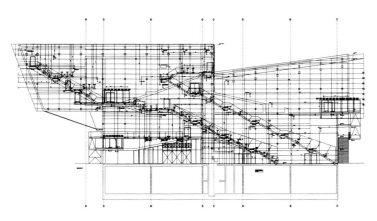
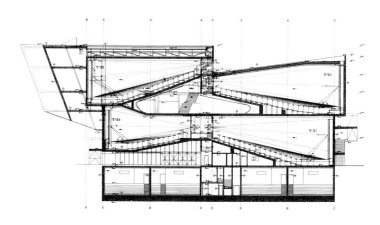
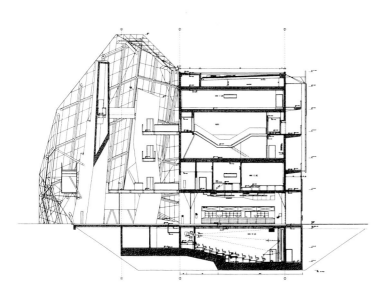
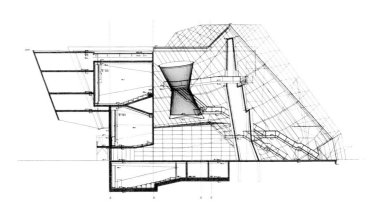

Interiors and sections

Trafford Centre, *Manchester*

FITCH

The slick, corporate chain cinema is well represented here by the international work of design firm Fitch. Featuring huge illuminated images from well-known movies, the lobbies, bars and circulation spaces of these cinemas become trailers for the main attraction and attempt a kind of universal corporate language. These images are recognisable almost throughout the cinema-going world, creating a ready source of branding within otherwise indistinct developer boxes or retail complexes. Schemes in Basildon and at the Trafford Centre in Manchester (both 1998) provide dynamic lobbies within exactly such undistinguished complexes, giving specific identities to areas within the building, in this case for UCI. Unashamedly commercial, these are spaces intended to sell consumers commodities in big quantities. Computer-game zones and popular fast-food franchises become big draws for local youths, turning the cinema into a desirable place to be with or without the film.

A central lobby, clearly delineated by a shallow dome, is the focus of public activity at the UCI Basildon. At the Trafford Centre in Manchester this central public space becomes the defining area of the building, a generator which throws off surrounding spaces centrifugally. At the UCI in Cardiff (1998), the central, circular space is made more tectonic with the insertion of a stair and a series of devices to break up the space, including monitors, seating, screens and angled, brightly coloured columns. This creates a series of more intimate bars and lounges – spaces less geared towards adolescents.

The round atrium as the generator of the public space reappears in the UCI Kinowelt Othsmarchen in Hamburg (1999). Escalators at skewed angles rise through the central atrium, influencing the forms of the concessions and a pair of curving bars while also creating a sculptural dynamic, visible through the fully glazed and highly transparent street frontage, which begins to suck audiences up through the building before they have even entered. Also in Hamburg, Fitch collaborated with German architects Von Gerkan, Marg und Partner on the even more transparent UCI Kinowelt, Friedrich Ebert Damm (1999). The attenuated, transparent elevation which displays the crowds of cinema-goers and the High-Tech roof structure, seems to resemble nothing so much as an international airport. Simple in plan and repetitive in detail, this huge cinema complex impresses through sheer scale, particularly at night when the illuminated building dominates its roadside site, becoming in itself a huge backlit billboard.

The Multikino in Poznan, Poland (2000), the country's first multiplex, has quickly become an institution where tickets for Saturday-night shows are resold on the black market for many times their face value. The cinema's exterior is a little austere, the blend of a few, rather weak High-Tech elements – a transparent facade and grey-blue tiles. But the interior is garish and colourful, and architecturally more interesting than the elevations would lead you to believe.

Fitch is also responsible for a pair of multiplexes in Japan at Inazawa and Niigata (both 1999). The latter of these two is enlivened by a dramatic and generous foyer space based around a pair of arcs in the plan. Although the space itself is squeezed into an undramatic developer's box, the architects have tried hard to create some spatial drama.

The same blown-up images from cult films have been used throughout these interiors to create the branding which cinema chains are so desperate to achieve and to take advantage of their vastly familiar filmic back-catalogues. Ephemeral and kitsch, they nevertheless succeed in creating colourful and amusing interior spaces which cannot fail to catch the eye, even if there is a distinctly knowing consciousness of their trashy and exploitative nature. These are the successors to the lobby cards that were themselves a sub-genre of idol worship and brand recognition – only writ large.

*TOP LEFT: **UCI Trafford Centre**, Manchester*
*TOP RIGHT and BOTTOM: **UCI**, Cardiff*

TOP: **UCI Basildon**
BOTTOM LEFT: **UCI Basildon**
BOTTOM RIGHT: **UCI Cardiff**

UCI Kinowelt, *Friedrich Ebert Damn, Hamburg*

UCI Kinowelt

ABOVE: **UCI Othsmarschen**, *Hamburg*
RIGHT: **UCI Basildon**

UCI Trafford Centre

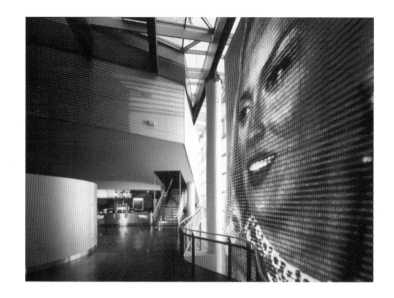

RIGHT: **UCI Othsmarschen**
BELOW: **UCI Trafford Centre**

TOP: **UCI Cardiff**
ABOVE: **UCI Huddersfield**
LEFT: **UCI Cardiff**

Screen, Winchester

FLETCHER PRIEST

For many years, a host of wonderful cinemas have been converted into buildings for other uses, from bingo halls to warehouses and even churches, while huge, dull multiplexes are built on sprawling suburban plots. But there have been a few cases where existing buildings have been converted into cinemas. One of the most unusual of these is a small Victorian garrison chapel in Winchester, which was converted into a local cinema by British architects Fletcher Priest Architects in 1996. The rather grim hall easily accommodated auditoria, which benefit from being kept in the dark. Screens are located at either end of the building with rakes rising towards the centre, where a single projection booth for both screens is located. Perhaps in reverence of its former military usage, the seats and walls are finished in a kind of khaki colour, while the truss roof was retained to maintain the original sense of space. Elsewhere in the building the walls are stripped back to their bare bones to expose raw brick, and new insertions are kept minimal and modern. Coloured lighting throughout the building creates a vibrant (though never garish) contrast with the earthy tones of the original structure. The interventions to the understated elevations are similarly subtle, with only the letters of the cinema's name (Screen) standing out from the original facade. Fletcher Priest has also been responsible for all the other Screen cinemas, operated by Mainline, throughout the UK.

It may seem tough to find a less sexy building type than a garrison chapel but a former hat factory in Luton provides fine competition. The Artezium (1998), set in the heart of hat country, is a pair of adjacent disused factories which have been converted by Fletcher Priest into an arts centre, incorporating a cinema as well as a theatre, bar and other facilities. The cinema is very different from the customary insulated box. Services and structure are left exposed and the utilitarian bench seats are accommodated on a steep

TOP: **Screen**, *Winchester*
BOTTOM: **Screen**, *Walton-on-Thames*

rake, creating the feel of a theatre rather than a traditional cinema – indeed the space is also used as a dance studio. An art installation by Tim Head entitled *Light Rain* is draped over one side of the auditorium, giving the effect of an intensely blue bead curtain and forming a visual link with the courtyard beyond the cinema wall, where its blue tinge reappears.

From the heady glamour of a Luton hat factory and an army chapel in Winchester, the move to the media bubble of London's Soho seems like a transition to another planet. The heart of the capital's film district hosts a pair of Fletcher Priest buildings catering to the industry. The offices for the Moving Picture Company (1999) are based around a post-production facility housed in a 1930s Art Deco building which was originally commissioned by the Rank Organisation. The 1930s elevations have been retained but the building was completely remodelled within to provide accommodation for studios, editing suites, special effects and production facilities, a café, conference area and seventy-four-seat cinema. The aim is to provide a buzzing, 24-hour environment in London's most vibrant late-night district.

Nearby, also in Soho, Fletcher Priest designed the new headquarters for Sony Pictures Europe in 1996. Built around an atrium and behind another retained street facade, the completely remodelled interior comprises screening facilities, technical and display systems as well as storage vaults and offices. Glass has been used extensively in the interiors to aid visual continuity, allow maximum penetration of light and moderate the physical presence of floors and stairs. In addition, daylight reflectors below the glass roof track the path of the sun and redirect light into the atrium and the working areas.

Artezium, *Luton*

The two highest-profile cinema schemes of recent years have undoubtedly been the auditoria at the Planetarium and the Science Museum. Both of these occupy the peripheral ground between cinema for entertainment and cinema for institutions, but their scale and interest make them worth considering in this selection.

London's is the most visited planetarium in the world. Its position adjacent to Madame Tussaud's, the famous waxworks with the equally famous queue, assists greatly in its popularity and it was to improve and rationalise the connection between the two buildings that Fletcher Priest were approached. A high-tech Digistar II star projector was fitted, the first in Europe, and seating was rearranged from the original circular layout to a front-facing arrangement. The entrance was reconfigured as an enamelled steel drum, which acts as a counterpoint to the building's trademark copper dome and creates a new interactive multimedia visitor area.

The new 3-D IMAX at London's Science Museum is another major intervention into the fabric of a genuinely popular and internationally recognised institution. It is the centrepiece of a dramatic new extension to the Museum, the Wellcome Wing. The cinema looms in space like an enormous UFO hovering above the ground, an image compounded by the escalator that appears from a hatch in its underbelly. You almost expect tacky tin-foil-clad aliens to come out declaring that they come in peace. Instead, audiences ascend, arriving behind and under the screen so that the scale of both the cinema and the film format is dramatically and suddenly revealed. A lightweight tension skin over the top of the cinema ensures that it is a pivotal and eye-catching presence within the new space.

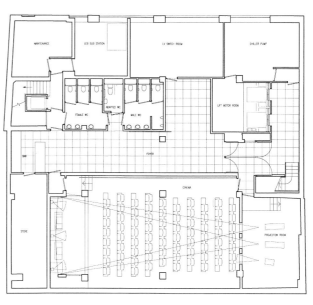

TOP: **Moving Picture Company**, *Soho*
BOTTOM: *Plan*

Sony Pictures Europe, Soho

Sony Pictures Europe

London Science Museum, IMAX

London Science Museum, IMAX

TIM FOSTER

The Tricycle Theatre is one of London's most adventurous and buzzing venues. It was designed by British architect Tim Foster in 1980 with a stripped-down and intimate auditorium which has been recognised as one of the most effective performance spaces in operation in a city where the competition is tough. The cinema is part of a programme of development for the site and is a way of supplementing the revenue of the theatre as well as opening up the building to a wider cross-section of the local community. Its construction allowed for a rationalisation and expansion of the front-of-house spaces and provided a cool new bar and foyer which serve as an antidote to the garish popcorn and hot-dog approach of most modern cinema foyers. The foyer area is brought forward onto the street with a glass box projecting into the public realm. This completely transparent entrance area is sheltered by the generously overhanging eaves of the portico. The cinema itself is expressed to the street in a severe blind box of brick, which is contrasted with the lighter steel and glass structure of the new studios perched above it.

The cinema auditorium is positioned in the basement, a fact revealed externally by a garish dash of red wall to the stairs, visible through a plate-glass window. In a welcome departure from the usual lack of attention paid to the architectural form of the auditorium, the Tricycle's interior is made memorable by a series of interlocking slanting planes, behind which light shines from unseen sources, illuminating the points where the planes overlap. The impression recalls the streamlining of late Art Deco interiors, where the eye was attracted to the screen by a series of wavy sections and mouldings. The angularity and the slanted geometry of the walls, however, brings to mind the early experiments of Expressionism (both on and adjacent to the screen), in which jagged forms and brilliant combinations of light and shadow hinted at mood, atmosphere and movement. Even the windows for the projector and projectionist in the rear wall have been treated in a sculptural, creative way, positioned within a frame so that they become elements within a light sculpture.

The Tricycle

The Tricycle

Credit Card
Collections

The Tricycle, *auditorium*

CINEMAS 電影院 1-5 ①
CINEMAS 電影院 6-11 ① →

AMC Festival Walk, Hong Kong

GENSLER

Based in Los Angeles, Gensler is a powerhouse of modern cinema design and architecture for all aspects of the movies. Their massive portfolio of work would be impossible to cover comprehensively in a brief summary so I have concentrated on a few of the schemes and illustrated more.

The most dramatic of Gensler's recent projects have been for AMC. Located within a shopping mall, the AMC Festival Walk scheme in Kowloon, Hong Kong, relies on the quality of the interior to set up the character of the cinema space. The main lobby is fragmented through a series of architectural devices, from dramatically modelled ceilings, columns and monitors to screens suspended from steel gantries. Skewed, sloping walls and surfaces address the escalators and introduce a three-dimensional dynamic to the lower levels, as well as acting as angled billboards. Curving metal rails and struts fly out below the ceiling at jarring angles, leading the eye around the space. This volume is preceded by a calmer, more expansive lobby, which forms the interface between the transport hub below the mall and the frenetic world of images, lights and jarring angles in the lobby above. The ticketing lobby serves eleven cinemas, crammed tightly into a city where space is never wasted.

Japan, too, is famous for its aversion to space-wasting and Gensler have constructed another AMC in a mall in Nakama on the island of Kyushu, 500 miles south-west of the Japanese capital. The complex consists of sixteen auditoria, all accessed from an entertainment building within an open-air mall. As at Kowloon, there was no opportunity to express the character of the cinema on the elevations, and it was left to the architects to construct the entire atmosphere of the complex in the lobbies and communal areas between the auditoria, but the feel is calmer, more transparent and less frenetic. There is a kind of sci-fi futuristic feel to the dramatically lit glass walkway and the brightly coloured, skewed planes. Angled handrails and grids add an extra dynamism and sense of movement to the circulation spaces. Huge beams and the underside of one of the walkways (which acts as a massive light-fitting) mould and sculpt the volumes of the lobby and ticketing spaces and prevent the customary darkness.

The designs for the Sony Theater, Lincoln Square, on New York's Broadway (within a shell designed by Kohn Pederson Fox) aim to create a Sony flagship comprising twelve auditoria and one nine hundred-seat cinema as well as a large-format IMAX cinema. The huge lobby is opened out to the street with a kind of multi-storey shop-window effect so that the activity, scale and colour of the interior become the building's billboard. A three-storey-high mural – a dazzling Art Deco pastiche – enlivens the escalator ride up to the cinemas and provides a visual key from the street. This mural motif has since become a popular tool within the often sterile glass box of modern cinemas. Although austere and slightly flat in elevation, the building comes to life in its colourful, often garish interiors. The auditoria themselves are as lavish and star-studded (literally) as the lobbies.

Gensler's intimate knowledge and massive experience of architecture for the movies has also won them a large number of commissions from industry insiders. Among their most interesting schemes are their designs for production facilities – the behind-the-scenes stuff which carries a certain voyeuristic interest for us outsiders.

AMC, Nakama

Sony Pictures acquired the MGM studio lot in Culver City, California, and were keen to exploit the nostalgia associated with the site. Gensler were commissioned to masterplan the complex and design eleven new cinemas, as well as restaurants, filmable facades, production facilities and offices. Permeated with a kind of Deco nostalgia for what is invariably perceived as Hollywood's golden age in the 1930s, there is a small-town feel to some parts of the site, and a decidedly Hollywood feel to other aspects of the buildings. Gates and entrances set up key trademarks and display an acute awareness of the importance of branding, as well as an odd insecurity about the modern in favour of the past. The theatres themselves are saturated with a kind of Beverley Hills villa chic, an amusing Californian stylistic mishmash of the tacky and the overtly extravagant.

There is a similarly eclectic mix of Deco and a kind of colonial Classical at the dubbing studios designed for Warner Bros in Burbank, California. Here the interior of the cinema is the focus of the scheme and is finely articulated rather than being left as a blank box. The masterplan for the Paramount Pictures Corporation lot in Los Angeles includes a luxurious cinema designed in a more contemporary vein, its amphitheatre form being reflected in the staggered curves of the ceiling. The curved forms reappear in the lobby in the undulating mouldings of the walls, stairs and ceiling. The post-production studios and screening rooms for Twentieth Century Fox, also in Los Angeles, are executed in a thoughtful modern manner, with an attention to detail which is unusual in a spatial type where darkness is too often used as an excuse for lack of architectural expression.

AMC, Nakama

OPPOSITE and ABOVE: **Sony Theatres**, New York

ABOVE and RIGHT: **Sony Pictures**, Los Angeles

ABOVE and LEFT: **Columbia Pictures**, *Los Angeles*

Warner Bros Pavilion, *Burbank*

Warner Bros Pavilion, *Burbank*

ABOVE and RIGHT: **Paramount Pictures**, *Los Angeles*

ABOVE and RIGHT: **Paramount Pictures**, Los Angeles

Fox-Little Theatre

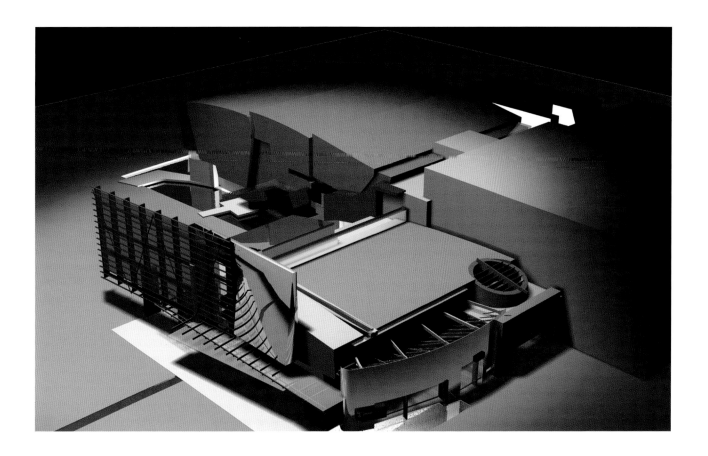

ABOVE and BELOW: **Kodak Theatre**, *design*

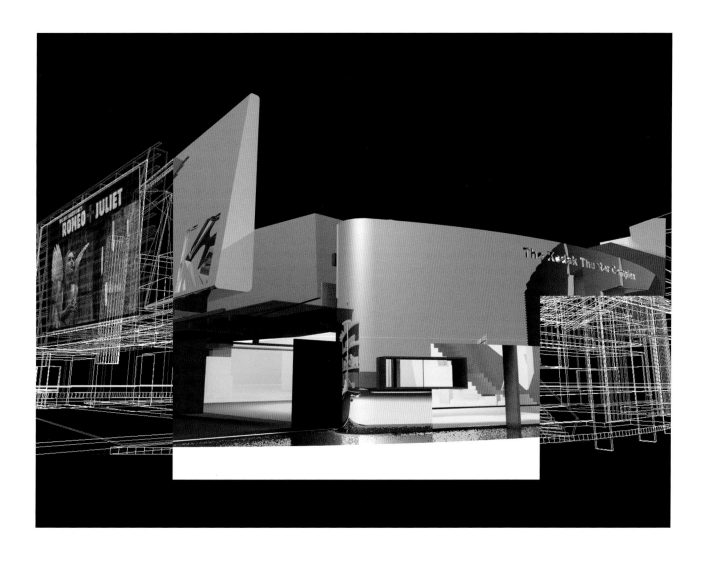

GEOFF MALONE INTERNATIONAL

The prolific work of Australian-born, Singapore-based Geoff Malone is a phenomenon in cinema architecture. As founder of the Singapore International Film Festival and someone who is passionately interested in film, particularly the sci-fi genre, Malone has had a powerful impact on the architecture of the region. His buildings have encouraged the pace of the spread of multiplexes throughout Asia and have administered a dazzling shock treatment of colour and light to the centres, outskirts and malls of a host of Asian cities.

The building that sparked off his practice's success in the cinema world was Yishun 10, the first multiplex in Asia, set in a suburban public housing estate in Yishun, Singapore. This bold, colourful, metallic fantasy was designed to enliven the housing estate and supply it with a throbbing, unapologetically commercial, public heart. Ten screens combine with huge video-walls and fast-food outlets to make this a genuinely popular local centre. Certainly there is nothing subtle about the design; this is a big box stuffed full of blindingly garish lights, which bathe the interior in candy-sweet pink and reddish hues. The internal details, like those on the outside, are High-Tech and mechanistic, with an occasional touch seemingly inspired by the Japanese fantasies (or sci-fi urban nightmares) of Shin Takamitsu. They are, however, stripped of any of the apocalyptic foreboding of Takamitsu's works. This is good-time stuff – no time for *Metropolis* fantasies of oppressive machines: these mechanistic motifs are pink, cuddly and, frankly, enjoyably stick-on. The populist atmosphere is clearly expressed by the neons, the buzz of the crowd and the sheer scale of the circulation spaces, foyers and unusually colourful auditoria.

The Savoy Cinema in Jurong, Singapore, is a conversion of an existing building. Here, the aesthetic is a candy-coloured, rose-tinted neo-Deco with heavy hints of early 1980s Memphis designs and the

extravagantly coloured Post-Modernism of Ettore Sottsass. Working within the rigid fabric of the original, relatively unmalleable shell, the architects created an internal language of odd shapes and gaudy colours, giving a kind of summery, Florida feel to the structure in a surprisingly effective jazzing-up.

The Tiong Bahru multiplex offers a slightly more subdued interior with seemingly expressionistic touches in the murky darkness behind the usual pink hues of the neons. Situated within a city-centre Singapore mall, the Tiong Bahru, like the Yishun 10, is set in a public housing estate and serves, at least in part, as a tool of regeneration and a vehicle for the creation of a public space.

Another Singapore multiplex, the Junction 8 at Bishan, creates a more colourful environment, with spacey effects and dynamically sculptural elements introduced into even the auditoria to produce a varied, constantly changing backdrop. The laser-battle and starship ceilings are a foretaste of what was to come at the Tampines, where Malone finally unleashed his full sci-fi sensibilities.

The Tampines multiplex is, like the Tiong Bahru, situated within a mall, but in a new-town shopping centre. Distributed over two of the mall's levels, it allowed the architects the luxury of high ceilings but with the downside of a lack of human scale. This latter problem was addressed with the insertion of a lightweight suspended dome, pierced with parabolic arches in such a way as to reveal the height of the volume beyond. Moving images can be projected onto the dome. The whole thing is permeated with the kind of UFO aesthetic that has become characteristic of Malone's work – the architect's love of sci-fi glows through in the delightfully B-movie details. There is a Saturday-morning, Flash Gordon spaciness about the fittings, from the suspended, neon-ringed globe which

Above and page 136: **Tampines Multiplex**, *Singapore*
Yishun 10, *Singapore*

forms the centrepiece (Malone's equivalent to the chandeliers that dominated the old movie palaces) to the star-speckled ceiling, glass tube lighting and shiny metallic balls. The kitsch, Space Age-retro look presaged Page + Steele's Toronto Colossus.

Although GMI have built prolifically in Asia – with the range of their cinema schemes encompassing not only Singapore but also Korea, Hong Kong, Taiwan, Thailand and even China – they have also built cinemas in Europe. The dynamic elevations of the Maroussi multiplex in Athens provided an opportunity to design the building's shell – a chance that appears only very rarely in the tightly hemmed-in sites of Asia, or in the many cinemas squeezed into malls and beneath office developments. At the Maroussi, the usual multiplex box is disguised by a series of protruding architectural elements which create canopies around the building. Attention is focused on the entrance by its placement within a glass tube, flaring out towards the top. The circular geometry of this tube sets up the shape of the foyer, a circular space centring on a star-shaped ceiling light. Another Mediterranean cinema scheme can be seen in the designs for the conversion of an enormous and architecturally striking industrial complex in Ostia, Italy. The original building was a splendid railway carriage factory dating from the Fascist era.

The most intriguing of Geoff Malone's designs was made in collaboration with Tom Kovac. The French Generic Cinema is a futuristic design for a free-standing multiplex which envisages the incorporation of a bookshop, restaurants (both fast and fine foods) and games areas within a coherent environment based around a series of cinemas showing all types of film, from art-house to blockbusters. The proposed cinema is the diametric opposite of the developer's box tarted up with bits of interior design. Instead, Malone and Kovac envisage a series of interiors flowing into one another. Fluid and organic, there are few distinctions between floors, walls and ceilings. All surfaces, whether glazed or solid, are pixelated screens with the capacity to display commercials, trailers or information, so that the architecture itself becomes the screen. The cinema spaces see the ceilings swooping down towards the screen so that the whole space becomes a kind of proscenium within which the audience is embraced – the arches seem to hint at the Deco luxury of the Radio City Music Hall.

This kind of biomorphic architecture seems to be presenting itself as a possible, intriguing future for the cinema. In such a future architecture and medium would unite in an integrated, seamless environment in which technology, structure, amenities and film are expressed as part of an expressive, free-flowing whole. Malone is one of the few architects who seem to be considering the cinema as a building type with great potential for change.

Yishun 10

OPPOSITE and TOP: **Savoy**, Singapore
BOTTOM: **Bishan**

Tampines Multiplex

Maroussi, Athens

Maroussi, Athens

ABOVE: **Bishan**
OPPOSITE: **Tampines**

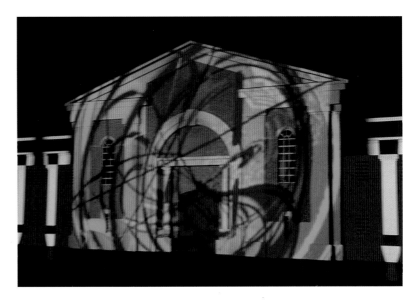
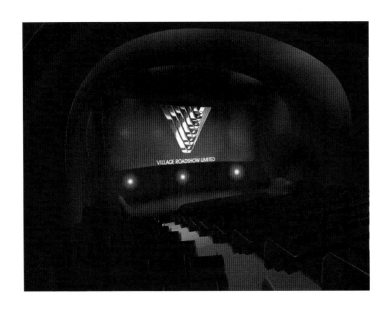

*LEFT: Designs for **French Generic Cinema***
*RIGHT: Designs for **Cinema at Ostia**, Italy*

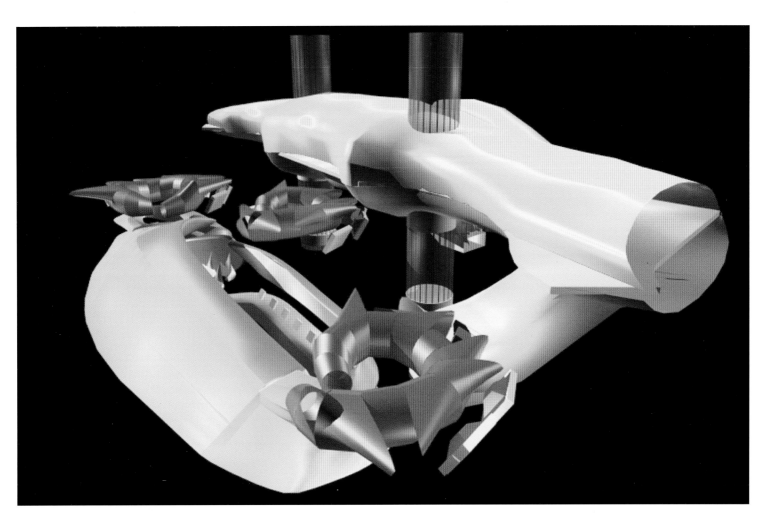

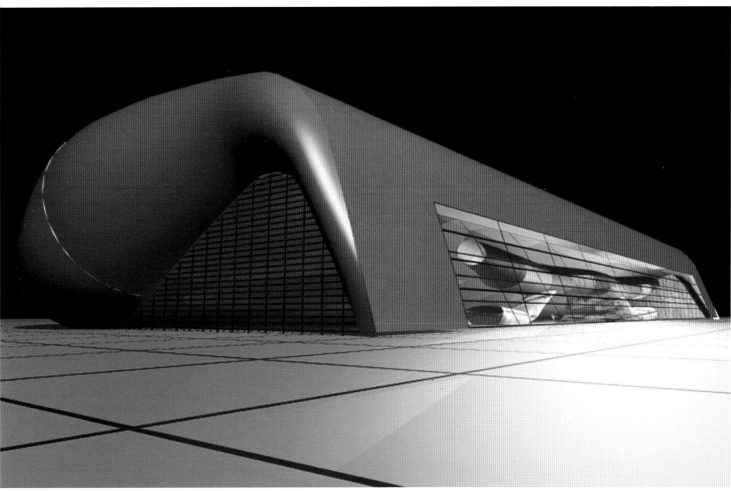

French Generic Cinema

JON JERDE

American architect Jon Jerde made his international reputation with a few huge schemes that blend urbanism with entertainment, creating whole quarters devoted to retail and commerce. His work is at once brash, kitsch and brazenly commercial yet often brilliantly conceived. He is the architect who has learned better than anyone else the lessons of Robert Venturi's late 1960s publications. Jerde has also learned from Las Vegas and introduced both complexity and contradiction into his corporate meta-worlds, which have an undeniable vibrancy. His approach works best when applied to landscapes that have become dysfunctional in human terms – urban areas blighted by depression or bad planning, no-man's-lands alongside motorways, post-industrial landscapes with the centres and the *raison d'être* sucked out of them. He was the perfect choice to create a vibrant, stimulating development for Europe's biggest cinema complex on the edge of Birmingham.

If it is fair to say that, broadly, there are two approaches to the modern cinema – the out-of-town box and the funkier, more self-conscious, city-centre cinema – then Jerde has created a third way. I hesitate to use the word 'environment', yet it is the word that springs to mind – Jerde creates a holistic environment for the cinema, a world that feeds off corporate recognition and familiar images, but nevertheless a world in which the architecture and the spaces count.

The Star City Complex (2000), designed in conjunction with Warner Village and UK architects Geoffrey Reid Associates, features thirty screens and a huge array of retail and leisure facilities and aims to cater for cinema-goers of all ages and tastes. Whereas other multi and megaplexes tend to cater for specific audiences, Star City provides bookshops along with the fast food, and screens Bollywood and art-house alongside blockbusters in a way that is still unfamiliar in the UK.

Jerde claims that the steel and masonry elevations of the new cinema were inspired by the industrial buildings and warehouses lining the canals around the site. The enormous lobby, however, takes its inspiration from West Coast, USA. It is adorned with a sprawling mural, the work of Ed Strang, a renowned production artist who was brought over specially from Burbank Studios. The painting sets up the semi-mythical Hollywood story using images from film and the kind of dark, non-specific metropolis backdrop familiar in films from Tim Burton's *Batman* to Ridley Scott's *Blade Runner*. This is blended with unconventional images of studios and stars and a fascinating *trompe l'oeil* effect of backlighting windows and signs. Jerde complements this melange with projections and trailers to create one of the most original and lively lobbies of recent years. Another of the complex's cavernous lobbies, set within a tapering cylinder, seems reminiscent of the nightmare ending of Terry Gilliam's future vision, *Brazil*. Star City's sprawling, neon-decked exterior blends images from Las Vegas with the streamlined, neon-lit towers familiar from the Moderne theatres of the 1930s and 40s, while also incorporating the imagery of S Charles Lee and the lights of a Japanese city centre.

OPPOSITE: **Star City**

Star City builds upon the success of other film-based Jerde schemes, including the masterplanning for Universal City Walk and AMC The Block 30 in Orange, both in the California heartlands of the film industry. Both schemes aim to create an urban atmosphere, with public spaces where walking and mingling is enjoyable and colourful, and car-free plazas for a state suffocating under the weight of its traffic and the ensuing smog. By thinking in these terms, Jerde is accepting the megaplex not merely as a giant mall, a climate-controlled box of franchises, but as a tool to recondition an entire culture into the pleasures of strolling and, as if encouragement were needed, shopping. His paradoxical mix of commercialism and art, of in-your-face franchising and an architecture which is genuinely good fun, may well save the megaplex from extinction and entirely alter the way that the out-of-town entertainment centre is viewed.

ABOVE and OPPOSITE: **Star City**, *Birmingham*

Star City

OPPOSITE: **Star City**
ABOVE: **AMC The Block 30**, Cedar Rapids, Michigan

ATSUSHI KITAGAWARA

From its inception, the cinema has been defined by its facade. The public face of the building has to serve as billboard for both the theatre, advertising its presence, and the films being shown within. The facade has often been the sole vehicle for the architect's vision, and the type of cinema with which we are still overly familiar is the blind box with a fancy-dress front. If one building has succeeded in dragging the modern cinema out of that architectural hole, it is Atsushi Kitagawara's bizarre box of tricks, the Rise Cinema in Shibuya, Tokyo (1983).

Dealing with a building type so reliant on a single elevation, cinema architects have tended to ignore the roof as an expressive element. The Rise Cinema is itself a single absurd roof which billows, twists and lifts to reveal a half-hidden world of the unexpected. The most striking element within the new roofscape is a gleaming metal curtain, which is drawn to one side to expose the harsh receding planes of the corner above the entrance. A smaller version of the metallic curtain appears beneath the canopy to create an overblown, theatrical box office which draws the curious into a dream-like interior world.

The stage-set absurdity of the exterior continues within as the visitor is drawn through a series of dramatic spaces tightly knit into one another. Walls and ceilings (some gently undulating) are distorted and skewed and interrupted by elements which fly across the space above them. Crystalline skylights jar with Rococo mirrors while industrial gangways and steel I-beams disrupt the voids above theatrically darkened foyers. It seems as if the architect is trying to match in the physical fabric of the building the distortions of space and time available to the film director. Kitagawara uses the architectural language of the film set – Baroque, impermanent, radically and fashionably Post-Modern – rather than the conventional palette of the builder. He is never bound by the constraints of convention or tradition that have tended to enthral the architects of the cinema.

The exotic architecture that cloaks the exterior and the foyers is taken right through into the auditoria – so often ignored by designers. One of the two auditoria is below ground, its subterranean location revealed by a layer of exposed rock which acts as a cornice between the top of the fragmented wall and the blackness of the ceiling. Here too, the characteristic cast-aluminium curtains drape surreally over the edge of the screen and glint in the flickering light of the projector, contrasting with the rich, plush red of real curtains tied with luxurious golden braids. In every space and on every surface Kitagawara plays with the contrast of softness and hardness, of highly finished colourful surfaces and the stark greyness of industrial materials. The building is spatially inventive and varied, from the striking elevations and memorable roofscape to the darkest corner and circulation space. Occasionally its dramatic language becomes overbearing, but it remains fascinatingly engaging. Intriguing, garish and self-consciously witty and theatrical, it seems the ideal entrance to the alternative world of the screen.

OPPOSITE: **Rise Cinema**

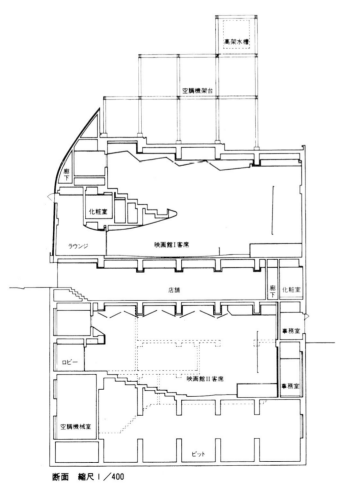

断面 縮尺 1／400

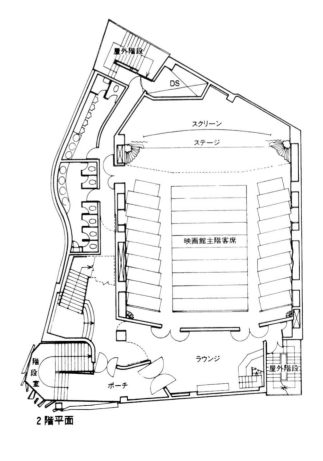

2階平面

Rise Cinema section and plan

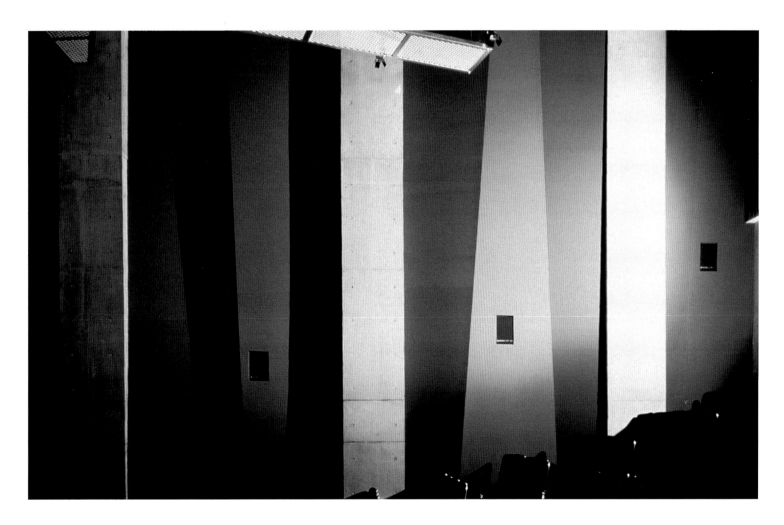

Designs for **Palazzo Del Cinema**, Venice

FUMIHIKO MAKI

In 1990 a competition was launched to revamp the home of the Venice Film Festival on the Lido. The original, now rather jaded building dating from the 1930s (remodelled in the 1950s) was to be retained and the centrepiece of the new building was to be a plaza accommodating an outdoor cinema. The entries that prompted the greatest interest and praise were those by Aldo Rossi, whose floating theatre for the Venice Biennale of 1980 remains one of the most poetic icons of Post-Modernism, and by Japanese architect Fumihiko Maki. In a fascinating manner the two designs seemed to encapsulate the Western and Eastern traditions of building.

Rossi's scheme was heavy and slightly lumpen. There was more than a hint of the monumental about it, and its scale and the repetitive rhythm of its facade echoed the Neo-Classicism of the Fascist architecture that prevailed when the original Palazzo del Cinema was built. Maki's submission was virtually the diametric opposite of Rossi's heavy design. Transparent and crystalline, his complex building consisted of elements staggered and built up within a simple flat roof and contained within a glass structure like a giant aquarium. A huge screen at the heart of the covered plaza was the scheme's icon and its heart, visible from within and from without, due to the consummately penetrable glass walls. The existing auditorium was retained at the centre of the design with the end wall wrapping around its horseshoe-shaped plan in an apsidal form, designed to appear to rise from the water like the stern of a boat.

Despite the impeccable modernity of Maki's design and the minimal simplicity of the forms, there is nothing dry or humourless about it. The most whimsical element is an observation deck on the roof which sits in the middle of a huge, sculptural wheel. Mimicking the shape of a giant film reel, it adds a kitsch quality yet also helps to make a rather flat building into a landmark. In its transparency, in its lightness in the townscape, and in the way it addresses public space, Maki's design anticipated both Koen van Velsen's Rotterdam cinema and Coop Himmelb(l)au's Dresden cinema.

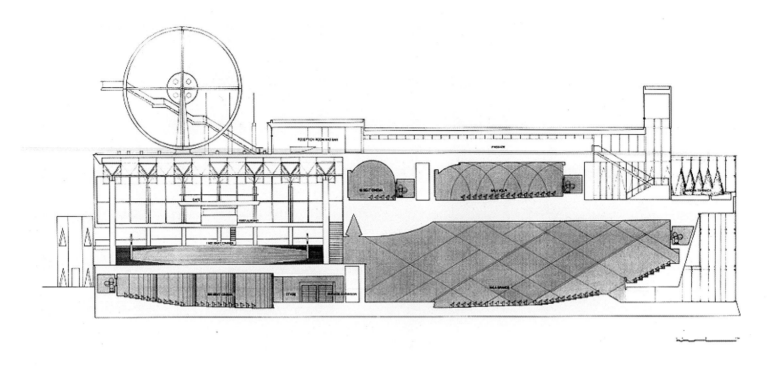

Section and plans

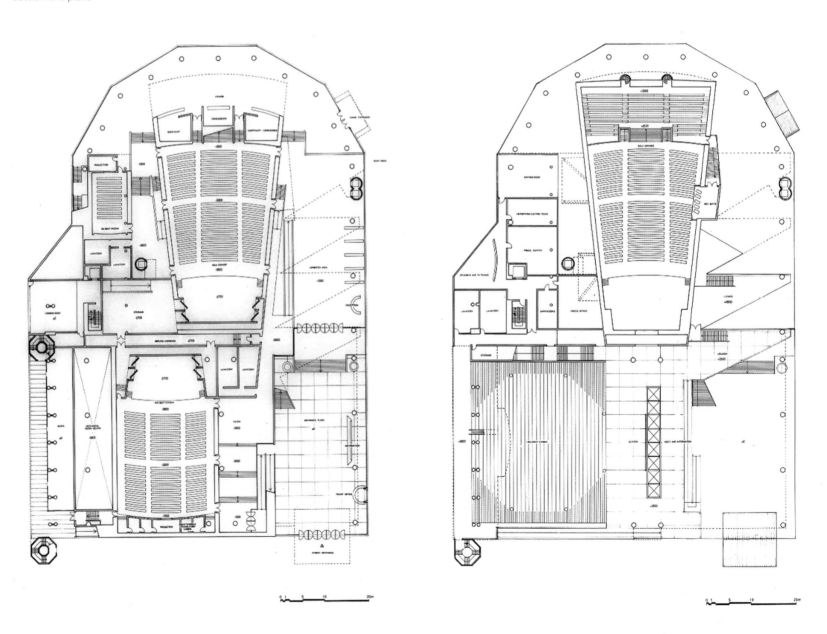

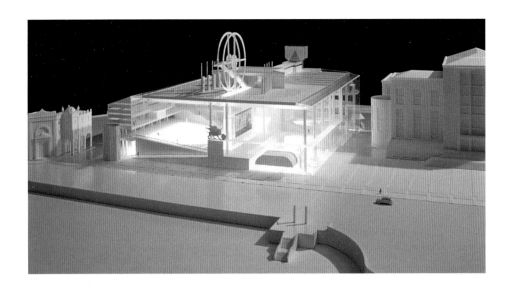

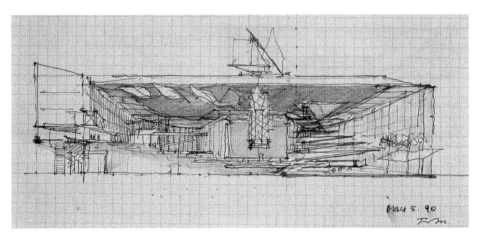

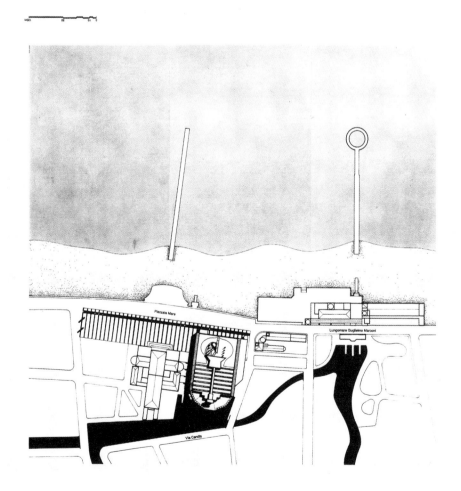

Model, sketch section and site plan

Colossus, Toronto

PAGE + STEELE

Canada is the home of the megaplex. Its cinemas are increasing in size at a seemingly unstoppable rate. The race for screen space has recently been clearly demonstrated on the outskirts of Toronto by a battle to the death between two giants of film distribution, Famous Players and AMC. Two vast megaplexes face each other across a flat suburban desert. The undisputed winner of the contest for visual domination goes to a huge UFO glinting in the sun, a series of tacky lights revolving around the disk of its roof. This is the outrageous exterior of Famous Players' Colossus Cinema (1999), the world's first circular megaplex. Toronto architects Page + Steele were determined to break out of the traditional boxy shed which dominates the world of the out-of-town multi-screen theatre and the result is this building – enormously tacky but fantastically good fun.

There is no attempt at subtlety or architectural sophistication at the Colossus. The huge car park catering for visitors to the cinema's nineteen screens stretches out before the long, low-lying walls and the dramatically lit flying saucer, and the night-time effect is reminiscent of the drive-ins of the 1950s. Despite its brashness, there is an undeniable sense of event and excitement about the structure. At the entrance of the hovering film-set flying saucer the lobby is a remarkable concoction of Space Age kitsch and sci-fi quotes from High-Tech architectures both real and imagined. From the carpet woven into a representation of a circuit board to the robotic clamps looming over the ticket offices, this is a riot of escapism. The central franchises are grouped under a UFO canopy which helps to control them within the overall space and to unite the lobby around a central core. Above this structure stands a gantry and a series of illuminated elements as well as a mishmash of suspended sci-fi paraphernalia. Light beams and dramatic illumination both inside and out contribute to the sci-fi kitsch aesthetic. Services are deliberately left exposed to recreate the often *ad hoc* interiors of spaceships, and ducts and tubes proliferate throughout the corridors and the central space. Even the beer is pumped from a vat through a series of pipes which conspicuously penetrate and adorn the central lobby.

The flying saucer lobby sits at the heart of the plan with the theatres spread out to either side along two wings so that even the plan form resembles some kind of spacecraft. This keeps circulation simple and logical, each theatre being accessed from one of two corridors which continue the juvenile space-fantasy theme with dangling props and brutally High-Tech services. Tongue-in-cheek and fantastically entertaining, the Colossus rates among the most exuberant cinema buildings of recent years and is so popular that it has become a type in itself, currently spreading through North American cities.

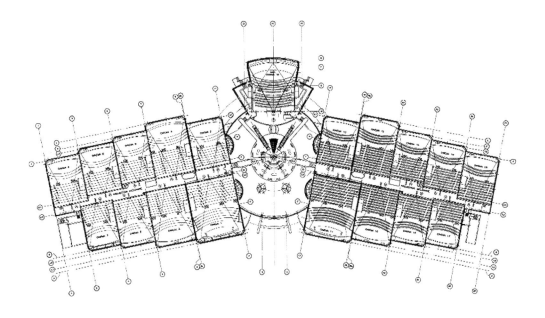

Colossus, *corridor and plan*

PANTER HUDSPITH

Just as the exodus of cinemas to the edges of towns was evidence of the urban decline that accompanied both recession and creeping suburbanisation in the 1980s, the use of the cinema as a tool of urban regeneration indicates a new approach to architecture, planning and the city. The polemics of Modernist planning and ideas about zoning ultimately led to the blandness of the out-of-town multiplex and the disassociation of architecture from the cinema building. Newer generations of architects have reinterpreted Modernist ideas and filtered out the failed, anti-urban gestures of their megalomaniac forebears. This new Modernism is urbane, elegant and happy to coexist with, rather than defy, its historical neighbours. The cinema architecture of British architects Panter Hudspith is a fine example of this emerging genre of urbane movie-house Modernism.

The designs for the City Screen Cinema in York (1999) aim to rejuvenate a stretch of the banks of the River Ouse. A three-screen art-house cinema forms the centrepiece of a broader redevelopment by the same practice, which encompasses a large bar, Internet café, restaurants, a conference room and a cantilevered riverside walkway. The scheme embraces an existing disused newspaper office, including the former printworks of the *Yorkshire Herald* newspaper, as well as newly built spaces, delicately interwoven with the Victorian and 1930s fabric of the existing structures. Despite the sleek, modern expression of the new buildings, the scale, colour tones and rhythms set up by the existing buildings are maintained using a few subtle touches: the bays and the rhythm of the structural columns of the café relate to the arcading of the neighbouring Romanesque Victoriana; and the blend of metal grids and large glazed surfaces is picked up in the new cinema buildings. These vertical expanses of glass allow cinema-goers to locate themselves within the city, giving views of the pair of churches that seems to sandwich in the building from either side. A wide staircase running through the heart of the complex knits in the old brickwork of the printworks with the smooth timber cladding of the new building, and creates a kind of alley, controlling circulation and resulting in a very urban interior space in which the old and the new are clearly differentiated yet subtly intertwined.

The refurbishment of London's Curzon, Soho (1998), is an example of a different kind of urban regeneration. Situated on Shaftesbury Avenue, a lively road known for Edwardian theatres and modern tourist tat, the brief was to create an oasis of urban art-house cool within a deeply uninspiring shell. The building dates from 1959 and is a fine example of the trend at that time to maximise development profits by subsuming a cinema into a monolithic office block. Panter Hudspith have turned the ground floor into a colourful, transparent bar with a Francophile *tabac* counter, which becomes the magnet for pulling people into the cinema. Once inside, bright colours, blond wood and spidery light-fittings create an arty, metropolitan blend, sometimes almost too slick. Downstairs the theme continues with comfy sofas and private nooks and niches, creating a series of highly social spaces which almost makes the three new screens (replacing the large single screen of the original) part of the background. This is cinema reinvented as a venue on the social scene.

OPPOSITE: **City Screen**, *York*

The utilitarian simplicity of the Clapham Picture House provides the antidote to the preening, media-land swank of the Curzon. Dating originally from 1991, the first part of the scheme was a simple conversion of an unspectacular existing building into a small art-house cinema. Glass blocks, a reused herringbone floor, and the simplest finishes create an air of unfussy solidity in what has become a fantastically successful cinema and a harbinger of a revival in the fortunes of a formerly rundown (if lively) area of South London. The second phase of the scheme, incorporating a new auditorium, has seen the cinema colonise the neighbouring building, while a wrap-around sign forming a new attic storey increases the cinema's presence on the street.

The Picture House at Stratford-upon-Avon (1997) was also slotted into an existing shell – another unglamorous building formerly functioning as a garage. Entered through a courtyard, a subtle canopy indicates the route which takes the user up a staircase to the main foyer. This, like the bar at the Curzon, Soho, is divided into public and more intimate social and bar spaces, with a café and terrace on another level above, which also houses the two auditoria.

Along with Burrell Foley Fischer and Tim Foster, Panter Hudspith are working successfully and consistently towards the reintroduction of cinema as a city-centre activity and social hub, a generator of urban renewal and the repair of the fabric of England's cities.

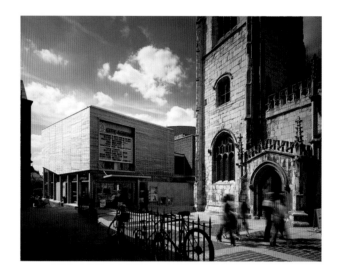

ABOVE: **City Screen**, York
OPPOSITE: **Picture House**, Stratford-upon-Avon

OPPOSITE and ABOVE: **Curzon**, Soho

RTKL

RTKL are specialists in big cinema complexes and the recent, fundamentally important shift from the predominance of the out-of-town multiplex to the big, urban cinema is very obvious in a few of the practice's recent designs. The design for Manchester's new works (2000) illustrates this change with a huge, city-centre complex in a converted printing works. The industrial aesthetic has been deliberately retained and, indeed, enhanced with extra touches (riveted girder bridges, bare brick walls etc.) in a move which attempts to achieve the same kind of grounding in the image of a city's local industrial history as WPH Architects achieved with their lumber mill aesthetic in their complex at Pacific Place, Washington. In effect, the Printworks is planned as a mall based around a cinema, the franchises garishly displayed all over its facades. This kind of mallification of the downtown cinema seems likely to become a feature of twenty-first century cinema architecture. The designs for Reading Cinemas in Australia echo the same semi-industrial aesthetic with their long, sculptural elevations composed of metallic planes and bolted-together masts and pylons.

The Warner Bros Central Cinema in Oberhausen, Germany (1996) is a return to the more familiar out-of-town multiplex. Centred around a glass tower and surmounted with a WB logo atop a High-Tech mast, the building is reminiscent of the roadside cinema architecture of the 1950s, architecture stripped down to its basic elements – sign and mass. A neon-clad canopy sweeps out from the glazed wall of the lobby, thereby tying together the two wings of the building and giving a foretaste of the light-show within. A ring of monitors and lurid neons forms a circle suspended at the centre of the lobby, giving the building its brilliantly lit heart.

Some of these same motifs are used inside the Warner Bros Cinema in Cheshire Oaks (1999). Here, neons and barrages of monitors and screens are wrapped around complex wavy gantries to create undulating spaces, their curves echoed in the solid designs of the franchise stand fronts. Similar purple and yellow surfaces and highlights define the interiors of the Warner Cinema in Portsmouth (2000).

OPPOSITE: **Filmworks**, *Manchester*
RIGHT: **Imax**, *Printworks, Manchester*

The UCI cinema in Norwich (1999) is a more sedate and adult affair. A gently curving roof is cantilevered a long way over the glazed wall of the lobby, creating a crisp edge. A single, slender column assists in stopping the paper-thin eaves from folding up. In contrast with the purplish glow of their Warner Bros buildings, the light here varies between a pale pink and a chill blue. A singular lack of neons, toned-down franchises, and a circular bar enhance the more adult feel of the cinema. At the centre of the lobby, one of the few franchises takes a star-shaped plan, its counter fronts strikingly illuminated. This form, which seems to generate the spaces around it, is best appreciated from the landings above. Its low-lying profile stops it from dominating the lobby but leaves the central atrium room to breathe and to revel in its height and light.

Among the most interesting of RTKL's recent designs is the ark-shaped building of the UCI KOH Cineplex at the harbour in Düsseldorf, Germany (2000). Picking up on the shape of hulls in the port, this unusual cinema has an almost sinister impenetrability. Alternating panels of dark and light cladding create a random, messed-up, checkerboard facade, which shields the building's interior. Its blindness indicates the necessity for darkness in the cinema space. This is a daring and unusual scheme which eschews the bright lights and pastel shades which more usually appear in RTKL's work.

TOP LEFT: *Imax*, Manchester
BOTTOM LEFT: *Filmworks*, Manchester
TOP RIGHT: *Warner Bros*, Cheshire Oaks
MIDDLE RIGHT: *UCI Norwich*
BOTTOM RIGHT: *UCI Koh Cineplex,* Dusseldorf

Warner Brothers Central Cinema, Oberhausen, Germany

ABOVE and BOTTOM LEFT: **Warner Bros**, *Cheshire Oaks*
BOTTOM RIGHT: **Warner Bros**, *Oberhausen*

SAUCIER + PEROTTE

Canada has recently become the centre for the development of the megaplex – the out-of-town or suburban super-cinema – in many ways replacing the USA, which has reached saturation point, as the home of bigness. Saucier + Perotte's fascinating little Cinémathèque Québécoise in Montreal (1997) is an example of a building which goes against the grain of suburban elephantiasis to provide an exquisite little urban cinema centre contained within a sophisticated series of interlocking spaces and sculptural forms.

The architects have taken a constrictive site between two existing structures and turned it to their advantage, incorporating a brick-built neighbouring school, which has been restored to house a film conservation centre. They are interested in instilling a sense of the movement of the city in the building's public aspects. The building itself becomes a series of compact urban spaces: squares, terraces and a bridge connecting the public realm outside to the cinematic realm within. A light-box forms the most striking feature of the main elevation and, as well as projecting pictures from films into the street, it is able to pick up images of movement (silhouetted figures) from within the building and periodically convey them to the city. The projecting screen is the outermost layer of a series of skins that makes up the elevation. Behind it, a gridded, glazed screen links the new building to the retained facade of the school and conceals shops, offices, a smaller cinema and the more private areas of the complex.

Along with movement it is light that interests Saucier + Perotte. To stress the dual meaning of the word 'light' in terms of weight and illumination, they have devised a series of playful moves: natural and artificial light are blended; the interior is both transparent and translucent in parts; and the lightweight steel structures of the interior are contrasted with the solidity of the stone facade and the rigidity of the retained Victorian facade next door.

The building also deliberately questions the wisdom of the conventional cinema as a blind box. As soon as the visitor enters, the foyer begins to break down the notion of a cinema space confined by rigid walls. Suspended above the entrance is a small balcony with raked seating which forms a canopy, reducing the scale of the double-height foyer and also creating a fully functioning screening space. The screen is suspended from the wall opposite the entrance and, as can be seen from the section, the space behind it is carved out to allow back-projection so that this becomes a kind of second light-box, echoing the feature on the facade. By placing screen and seating in mid-air, the cinema ceases to be a private, enclosed, darkened space and becomes an activity that is part of the public realm.

OPPOSITE: **Cinémathèque Québécoise**, *Montreal*
RIGHT: **Magnum Cinema**

Just as film consists of a series of images, of glimpses and scenes disembodied in time and space, so Saucier + Perotte have attempted to approach this building as a journey through a series of interlocking and interrelated spaces, from which both the past (the parts of the building you have already visited) and the future (those spaces where you are going or which are incidental) can be glimpsed simultaneously. The proliferation of glass inside and outside and the various effects of transparency and opacity heighten a sense of curiosity and stimulate the eye. The different kinds of light echo the phases of the cinema building, from the darkness of the auditorium to the beam of the projector and the dazzling glare of light after emerging from a daytime screening. At the same time, a courtyard with a garden and terrace café brings air and sky into the heart of the building, permeating the public spaces with natural light during the day so that they change with the movement of the sun. Acting as a lung, the trees and open air of the courtyard dispel the climate-controlled artificiality of most modern cinema architecture. Another small courtyard is created behind the film conservation studios. Complex, spatially inventive and thoughtful, the Cinémathèque Québécoise succeeds in bringing some of the versatility of film into architecture in one of the finest urban cinemas of recent years.

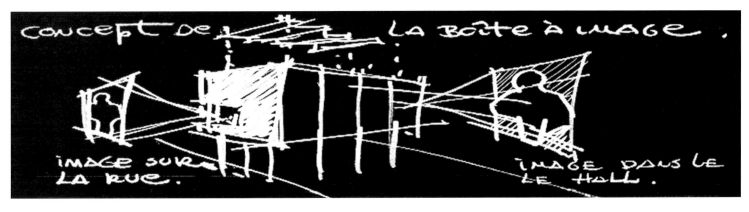

Cinémathèque; *MIDDLE: Elevation drawing; BOTTOM: Concept sketch*

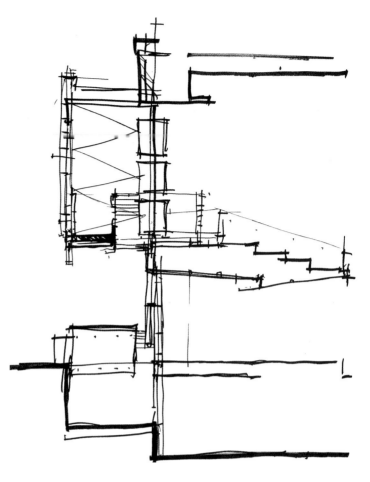

ABOVE: Sketch section

Verona Cinema Centre

TONKIN ZULAIKHA

Tonkin Zulaikha's Verona Cinema Centre in Sydney (1996) is part of a mixed-use development which incorporates residential, retail and office space, a café and even a yoga centre. Situated in a lively urban setting, it is a model development which makes use of the existing urban fabric (it is set into the shell of a 1940s industrial building) as well as creating its own cultural and urban blend in which the various uses all feed off and benefit one another.

The existing structure was a dreary two storeys of brick and concrete, but using that structure as the basis of the new building has allowed the architects to create a sculptural roofscape which seems to burst out of the confines of its surroundings. The skyline is dominated by the top of the stair tower, which explodes through the roof and binds together the disparate elements of the building below. This tower, particularly when illuminated at night, effectively becomes the cinema's billboard, announcing its presence in the streetscape.

Within the building, a series of skews and disjunctions allows the architects to weave the new structure and the four cinemas around the existing columns. The fragmentation is taken up within a pair of foyers, one open to the street, exposing the activity inside, and the other at a higher level, deeper within the building. The materials are more in line with the building's industrial past than with the garish commercial cinema tradition: finely finished concrete, stainless steel, extensive glazing, a copper-clad canopy and neon lighting give a functional feel. Rather than applied graphics, it is the light, spatial composition and highly sculptural internal massing which give dynamism to the spaces. There is even a touch of the functional, no-nonsense Australian vernacular in the roofscape of corrugated steel, glass and metal glazing bars.

The Norton Street Cinema (1998), also in Sidney, follows a similar pattern in that the front of the building is made completely transparent to the street and a tower marking the central stairs forms the key streetscape feature of the building. It is, however, a smoother, more urbane design. A clearer, more rational plan allows a neat distribution of the four auditoria, and the spatial drama is provided by the intersection of spaces and interpenetrating levels rather than by skewing or by dislocated grids. Again, the architects have used functional, workmanlike materials in an unusual way to create striking architectural forms from unlikely fabrics. The neons announcing the name of the cinema are stuck onto a long red-painted I-beam that cuts right across the street elevation. Industrial-looking materials also form the slender tower which denotes the entrance below and forms a dramatic billboard. The tower's structural fins and blend of vertical and horizontal dynamics recall the roadside pop architecture of the 1950s American drive-in and create an equally effective illuminated advert.

The interiors, too, are characterised by harsh, industrial materials, but these are used with such fineness and inventiveness that they cease to appear as found objects and begin to relate to the peculiarly Australian tradition of creativity with low-cost materials. Again the concrete, steel-beams and factory glazing pervert the customary cinema aesthetic. They are used to create fascinatingly complex spatial sequences which are occasionally reminiscent of the highly mannered Los Angeles work of Morphosis, blended with the less self-conscious, hard-wearing aesthetic of Glenn Murcutt. The unusual light-fittings, created from series of horizontal planes, break up the spaces in an interesting modern reinterpretation of the theatre-foyer chandelier.

Both buildings are refreshingly original, intelligently architectural, with space and light used as tools to generate the form of the structures, displaying a healthy disregard for the graphics-led aesthetic of the corporate movie industry.

Verona Cinema Centre and plan

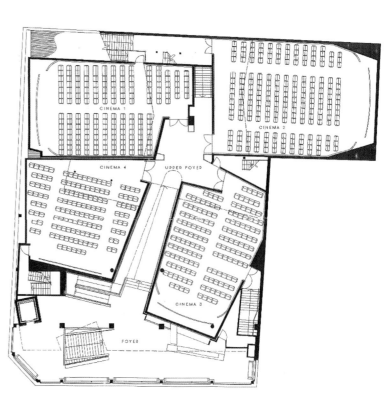

OPPOSITE and ABOVE: **Norton Street Cinema**

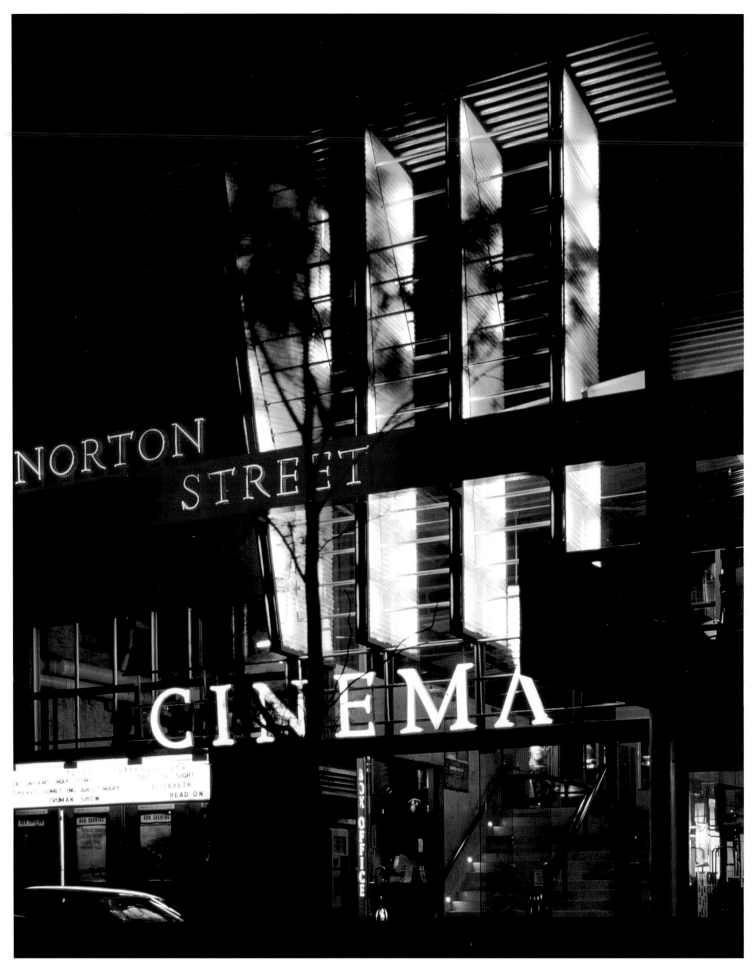

Norton Street Cinema

KOEN VAN VELSEN

Koen van Velsen's Pathé Cinema (1997) has reinstated the Schouwburgplein as the centre of Rotterdam's entertainment district. Set within the revitalised square, which has been strikingly masterplanned by landscape architects West 8, the cinema's sheer, lightweight walls form the perfect foil to the inventive surfaces of the square itself. Van Velsen has subverted the traditional image of a cinema as a solid block with an elaborate facade, by cladding his seven auditoria in a translucent envelope. The result is a structure that appears as light and practical as a mass-produced paper lampshade but adds a simple, minimal elegance to the square.

At ground level the building is completely transparent; plate-glass windows allow unimpeded views in and out of the interior from all around, but also give the appearance of a massive urban block floating above the square. The main entrance is at the northern end of the square (its siting takes into account the theatre building which sits opposite) and is formed by a very deep overhang which creates a kind of canopy. A colonnade of massive metal-clad columns leads into the box office area, which in turn leads via a grand staircase to a first floor which is devoted entirely to a huge, flowing foyer space. From here a complex but relatively transparent series of stairs ascends to the cinemas, introducing a three-dimensional dynamic to the foyer without detracting from the sense of openness and continuous space.

Opening up to the public realm all through the day, the interior changes radically at night. During the day the thin membrane walls admit a milky white light which bathes the interior spaces in an even glow. At night the polarity is reversed and light gently seeps from the walls to the public square outside. The cinema's appearance evokes that of Rafael Moneo's Kursaal Auditorium in San Sebastian, Spain, a glowing box illuminating the public realm.

If the membrane wall is comparable to a kind of skin which wraps around the building, then the cinemas themselves could be seen as the building's vital organs. Seven cinemas of varying sizes, accommodating audiences of between 200 and 700, are laid out in a sculptural arrangement, staggered both in plan and in section. Like a body, it is through the section that the internal layout can be most easily read. Three smaller cinemas appear on the ground-floor plan, the first-floor foyer is positioned above them, and above the foyer are the larger auditoria, their raked floors forming a jagged, sculptural ceiling. With each cinema acting as a separate architectural component, expressed as an individual form and separated by wells or barriers, the architect has avoided problems of acoustic leakage from cinema to cinema.

Van Velsen's approach represents a typically rational Dutch solution which combines a sparse, minimal elegance with a fascinating sculptural location of the elements once you are inside the building. Despite the size and volume of the structure, there is nothing megalithic about it. In fact it is remarkably self-deprecating during the day, its milky whiteness blending into the dull grey of Rotterdam's northern sky and the stony concrete colours of a very modern (self-consciously modern) city centre. By chamfering the corners of the building, the architect further reduces its mass and impact on its surroundings, while also helping the flow of pedestrian traffic around its sides. In its subtlety, intelligence and delicacy, van Velsen's cinema suggests an alternative approach to the familiar brick boxes and tin sheds.

OPPOSITE: **Pathé Cinema**

Pathé Cinema *and section*

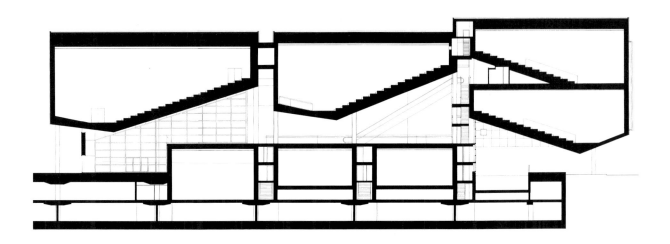

Plan

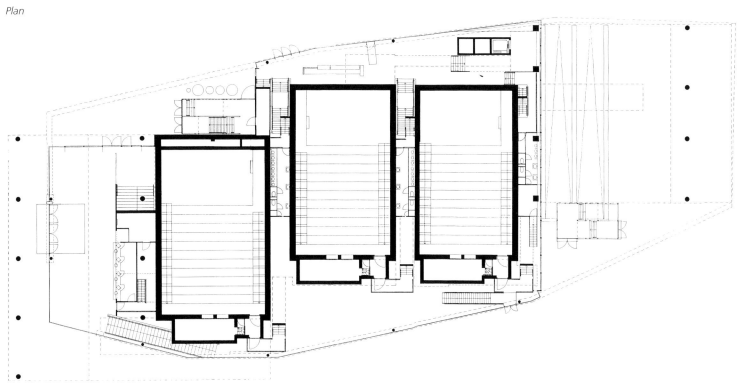

Evergreen Parkway 16

WPH ARCHITECTURE

Eschewing the easy route of cartoon characters, applied corporate branding and blown-up film stills, WPH Architecture has created a brilliantly varied *oeuvre*, combining avant-garde architectural motifs, arty neon designs and thoughtful, impressive spaces to create some of the most considered and refreshing of contemporary cinema buildings. Their work, scattered around north-west America, is marked out by a gritty urbanity, even though many of their designs are in suburban locations. Surfaces of block and brick, both inside and out, help to anchor these buildings to the ground and introduce a solidity and coarsely grained permanence which is rare in the ephemeral world of cinema design.

Architecturally these buildings are neither complex nor particularly radical, but they show a considered juxtaposition of natural materials with dramatic lighting and the industrial toughness of perforated metal. This makes for a striking blend of skeletal modern architecture with references to the dramatic skylines of Las Vegas and the classical age of US roadside cinemas. The attenuated masts and broad, illuminated canopies of their cinemas at Hillsboro, Oregon (1994, expanded 1998), Eugene, Oregon (1995), and Redmond, Washington (1995, expanded 1999), are typical of an American tradition which uses the building itself as a huge billboard. At night, the sweeping curves of the buildings' facades become huge roadside screens which both reflect the nature of the spaces within and allow glimpses of spectacular neon light-shows. These buildings, in common with most of WPH's cinema work, were commissioned by Act III Theaters, subsequently acquired by Regal Cinemas. In an industry obsessed with corporate identity, the practice's designs have helped to create a crucial and recognisable brand based on architecture rather than graphics.

Evergreen Parkway 16

Their second cinema at Hillsboro, Oregon (1997) and others at Wisonville, Oregon (1996), Las Vegas, Nevada (1997), and Spokane, Washington (also 1997), introduce another architectural element from the classic era of freeway building – the illuminated tower. In each of these schemes, the cinema itself is kept within an unpretentious shed. Using basic warehouse systems and a utilitarian architectural language (almost a non-aesthetic), the architects create buildings with a single focus that gives individual character yet allows for the economy of no-nonsense theatres. Although they vary a great deal in form, the towers on these four buildings share an essential language – that of the skeletal metal scaffold illuminated by an abstract composition of neon tubes. The illuminated linear forms of the Spokane Cinema create a kind of ghost structure, an architecture composed solely of light with no substance behind it. It is a fine metaphor for the shaft of light from the projector, which has no physical substance yet can convey emotion and infinitely complex narrative once projected onto the screen: the tower becomes a symbol of the intangibility of a medium created through light. There is even a hint of the Modernist church in these glowing neons; the primary colours and the hint of a cross in the abstract designs, together with the suggestion of a spire, hint at the mythical and ritual status of the cinema and its semi-sacred, mysterious shaft of light. In the case of the Spokane the architects created a series of grids on the elevations which themselves become screens on the street. The neons, arranged in abstract compositions that echo De Stijl aesthetics, appear in the darkness within as absurd stained-glass windows, miraculously producing a brilliant light from the darkness of the night sky beyond.

A similar motif of the jewel-like sparkle of neon within the darkness of an interior appears in the cinema in Gresham, a suburb of Portland, Oregon. Here, a low-budget box of a building is enlivened by pinpoints of brilliant coloured light which echo the windows of the projector booth but also imply a realm of illumination in the spaces beyond. The industrial steel gantries that form the elevations, and the ingenious use of signage affixed to perforated screens, lend the building lightness and yet allow it a significant and unmissable presence in the local landscape.

While much of WPH's work depends on creating landmarks in the streetscape or alongside a freeway, a significant part of it involves making space for cinemas within pre-existing malls and entertainment centres. To differentiate space for the movies within settings already suffocating under the weight of corporate signage and shop-window lights is no easy task. The Pacific Place 11 Cinema in Seattle, Washington (1998) represents an ingenious solution to the cinema in an over-branded setting. Referring to the area's lumber trade, the lobby is based around an eccentric forestry tower, its furnishings echoing the local fittings of lodges. Huge timbers hewn from trees left standing after forest fires create an internal landscape of coarse, natural materials which jolts the visitor from the artificiality of the mall experience. At the cinema at Bellevue, Washington (1999), audiences are drawn through the mall to a cinema three floors up via a projecting glass booth, its gridded glass walls illuminated in frames of brilliant blue neon.

WPH have made a trademark of incorporating signage into their architecture in such a refined way that the lettering becomes the *raison d'être* of the architecture and vice versa. In recent years perhaps only Tonkin Zulaikha has achieved similar effects, in the Australian urban landscape. This emphasis on the integral role of the sign in the elevation can be seen as a reflection on the ideas of *Lichtarchitektur* in 1920s Germany. A series of innovative signs at WPH's cinema in Kennewick, Washington (1997), uses both natural and artificial light projected onto the textured surfaces of the building. In this way the bland utility of an elevation of a suburban mall becomes a low-rent billboard advertising the building with no use of gaudy applied graphics. At the same time a complex screen is suspended from the elevation, brilliantly backlit to suggest the overflowing light of the auditoria and to cast striking, expressionistic shadows on the otherwise mundane wall.

Other cinemas at Tukwila, Poulsbo and Lakewood (all Washington 1999), use lively arcades and broad overhanging canopies to create sculptural elevations, with illuminated signage adding planes of light to already complex architectural compositions. The protruding fin of the Lakewood Cinema existing solely as a surface for the bright red neon characters, crowned by a green neon strip and pierced at ground level, is a strong and welcome echo of German *Lichtachitektur*.

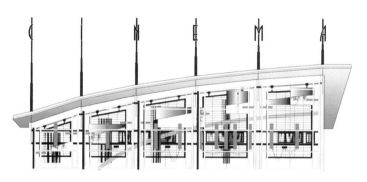

Cinema World 8, *Valley River*

Plan

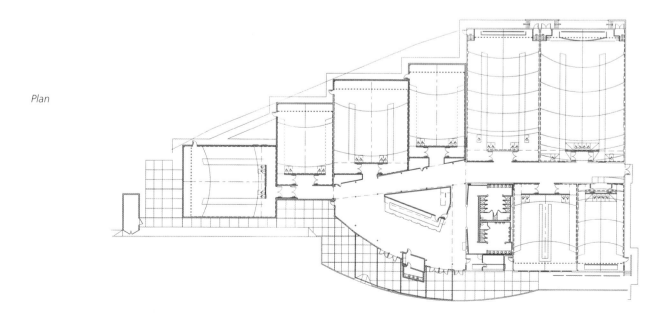

Bella Bottega 11

Movies on TV 16

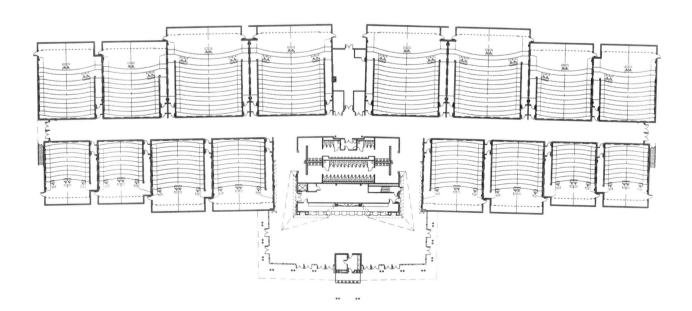

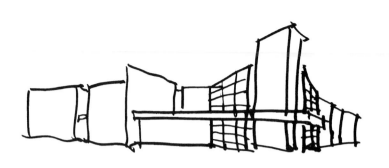

Spokane Valley 12 and plan

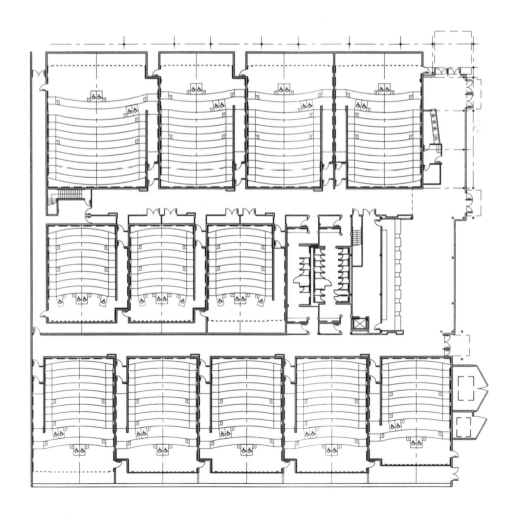

Stark Street 10

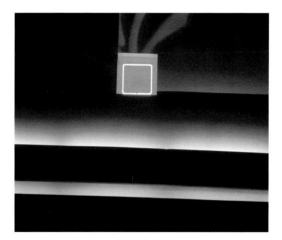

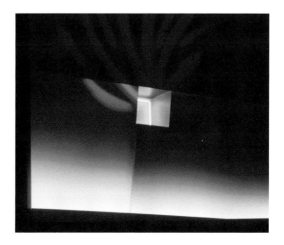

Pacific Place 11
*OPPOSITE: **Columbia Centre 8***

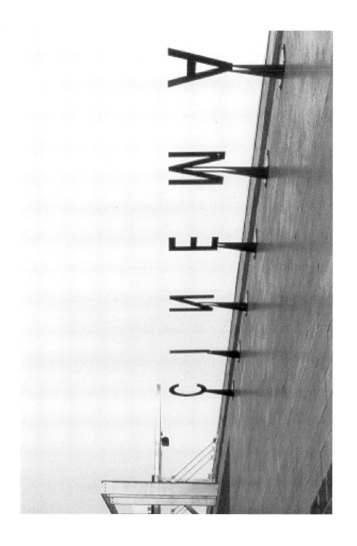

Parkway Plaza 12

TOP: *Lakewood 15 Cinema*
MIDDLE and BOTTOM: *Poulsbo 10*

BRIEF BIBLIOGRAPHY

Atwell, David, *Cathedrals of the Movies*, London, Architectural Press, 1980

Baacke, Rolfe-Peter, *Lichtspielhäuserarchitektur in Deutschland*, Berlin, Frölich and Kaufman, 1982

Bayer, Patricia, *Art Deco Interiors*, London, Thames and Hudson, 1990

Boeger, Peter, *Architektur der Lichtspieltheater in Berlin*, Berlin, Verlag Willmuth Arenhovel, 1993

Breeze, Carla, *LA Deco*, New York, Rizzoli, 1991

Bush, Donald J, *The Streamlined Decade*, New York, George Braziller, 1975

Cinema Theatre Association, *Gaumont British Cinemas*, London, 1996

Duncan, Alastair, *American Art Deco*, London, Thames and Hudson, 1986

Eyles, Allen and Skone, Keith, *London's West End Cinemas*, London, Keyton Publications, 1991

Furberg, Kjell, *The Picture Palace in Sweden*, Stockholm, Swedish Museum of Architecture, 1989

Gebhard, David, *The National Trust Guide to Art Deco in America*, New York, John Wiley, 1996

Gray, Richard, *Cinemas in Britain*, London, Lund Humphries, 1996

Hall, Ben M, *The Best Remaining Seats: The Golden Age of the Movie Palace*, New York, Clarkson N Potter, 1961

Lacloche, François, *Architectures de Cinemas*, Paris, Editions de Moniteur, 1981

Margolies, John and Gwathmey, Emily, *Ticket to Paradise – American Movie Theaters and How We had Fun*, Boston, Little, Brown and Co, 1991

Morton-Shand, P, *Modern Theatres and Cinemas – The Architecture of Entertainment*, London, Batsford, 1930

Naylor, David, *American Picture Palaces: The Architecture of Fantasy*, New York, Van Nostrand and Reinhold, 1981

Naylor, David, *Great American Movie Theaters*, Washington DC, The Preservation Press, 1985

Onderdonk, Francis S, *The Ferro-Concrete Style – Reinforced Concrete in Modern Architecture*, The Architectural Book Publishing Company, 1928, Reissued Hennessy and Ingalls, Santa Monica 1998

Pevsner, Nikolaus and Richards, J M, *The Anti-Rationalists*, London, The Architectural Press, 1973

Pildas, Ave, *Movie Palaces – Survivors of an Elegant Era*, New York, Clarkson L Potter, 1980

Richards, J, *The Age of the Dream Palace*, London, Routledge, 1984

Sanders, Don and Susan, *The American Drive-in Movie Theater*, Osceola, Wisconsin, Motorbooks International, 1997

Segrave, Kerry, *Drive-in Theaters: A History From Their Inception in 1933*, Jefferson, North Carolina, McFarland and Co, 1992

Sharp, Dennis, *Modern Architecture and Expressionism*, London, Longmans, 1966

Sharp, Dennis, *The Picture Palace – and other Buildings for the Movies*, London, Hugh Evelyn, 1969

Stones, Barbara, *America Goes to the Movies*, North Hollywood, National Association of Theater Owners, 1993

Valentine, Maggie, *The Show Starts on the Sidewalk – An Architectural History of the Movie Theater*, New Haven, Yale University Press, 1994

Webb, M, *Greater London's Suburban Cinemas*, Birmingham, Amber Valley, 1986

Weedon, Geoff and Ward, Richard, *Fairground Art*, London, White Mouse Editions, 1981

INDEX